THE BEST OF *WORKBASKET*® MAGAZINE

VINTAGE to VOGUE

35

Knit and Crochet Classics
Redesigned for Today

©2003 Krause Publications

Published by

700 East State Street • Iola, WI 54990-0001
715-445-2214 • 888-457-2873
www.krause.com

Please call or write for our free catalog of publications. Our toll-free number to place an order or obtain a free catalog is 800-258-0929, or please use our regular business telephone 715-445-2214.

Library of Congress Catalog Number: 2002105088

ISBN: 0-87349-421-0

Compiled and edited by Deborah Hufford.

Introduction

A great needlecraft magazine joins premiere yarn companies in recreating classic fashions from its last seven decades

When we first approached leading yarn companies with our concept for this book, they were intrigued. We had just purchased seventy years of archives from the world's once largest needlecraft magazine, *Workbasket*. As we perused its pages from as far back as the 1930s, we imagined how fun it would be to do a book revisiting some of its classic fashions and invite the world's most prestigious yarn companies to recreate the fashions. The yarn companies we approached were as excited as we were about the idea.

At its apex in the '90s, *Workbasket* was the largest needlecraft magazine in the world. First launched in 1935 during the Depression, it began as a modest little newsprint pamphlet called, endearingly, *Aunt Martha's Workbasket*. As its tagline "For Pleasure and Profit" implied, it provided readers not only leisure but a means to supplement their meager family budgets during those lean times. The diminutive digest became relied upon and loved by armies of avid needlecrafters over the decades. By the time *Workbasket* ceased publication in 1996, it had garnered a modern readership of many millions, and its end was mourned by generations.

To peruse the pages of *Workbasket* magazine's past seven decades is to experience time capsules in history. There were the jaunty hats and suits of the 1930s, and the bold, broad-shouldered 1940s fashions for women during World War II, when so many *Workbasket* readers were working in factories welding and riveting for the war effort. The 1950s brought new prosperity and prim fashions to go with it. The '60s and '70s brought Baby Boomer fashions that—surprise!—are the very styles being revived everywhere in retail stores today. Whatever the decade, timeless classics abound in the pages of *Workbasket* and underscore the adage, "everything old is new again." Thus, our title, *Vintage to Vogue*.

One aspect of fashion, however, *has* changed dramatically—the incredible array of textiles offered by today's yarn companies. The variety of colors, textures, weights, and styles available to needlecrafters today is nothing less than mind-boggling. No wonder needlecrafting is so popular again! We invited these premiere companies—Coats & Clark, Lion Brand, Berroco, Cascade, Tahki Stacy Charles, and Handy Hands, a leader in tatting—to participate in this book, with spectacular results!

Vintage to Vogue is packed with 35 projects of many styles, yarn types, and skill levels, all with complete, easy-to-follow directions. We've also provided a section of How-to Basics in Knitting, Crocheting, and Tatting, as well as a Resource section, containing product information, informative Web sites, and sources for free patterns, all for *your* pleasure! Aunt Martha would be proud...

1930s

1940s

1950s

1960s

1970s

1980s

1990s

VINTAGE to VOGUE

TABLE OF CONTENTS

Chi-Chi Shag

■ ■ ■

Workbasket's 1984 whisper-soft pullover is transformed into a sumptuous shag that shouts sensation! The contemporary sweater is knit in Tahki Stacy Charles' textural and irresistibly tony Casca yarn.

■ **PROJECT**
Sage Shag Pullover, by Tahki Stacy Charles

■ **SKILL LEVEL:**
Beginner

■ **SIZE**
Small (Medium, Large)
Directions for Small with larger sizes in parentheses.
If there is only one figure, it applies to all sizes.

■ **MATERIALS**
TAHKI STACY CHARLES Austermann Casca
13 balls (50 g balls, each approx 55 yds), in #05 Green

■ **NEEDLES**
Size 15 knitting needles
Size 10½ crochet needles

■ **GAUGE**
7 sts and 11 rows = 4" over Rev St st.
TAKE TIME TO CHECK GAUGE.

1984 Workbasket

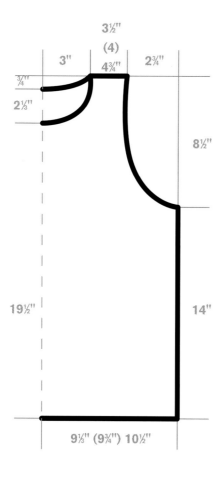

ABBREVIATIONS:

beg = begin, beginning; **bet** = between; **BO** = bind off; **CO** = Cast on; **dec** = decreas(e)(s)(ing); **inc** = increase(e)(s)(ing); **pat** = pattern; **rnd** = round; **rem** = remaining; **RS** = right side; **sc** = single crochet; **st(s)** = stitch(es); **St st** = Stockinette stitch; **tog** = together.

DIRECTIONS

BACK

Cast on 34 (36, 40) sts and work in St st until piece measures 14" from beg.

Shape Armholes: Bind off 2 sts at beg of next 2 rows, dec 1 st each side every 2nd row 3 times = 24 (26, 30) sts. Work even until pieces measures 22" from beg.

Shape Neck: Bind off center 8 sts and working both sides at once, bind off 2 sts from each neck edge once. Work even until piece measures 23" from beg. Bind off rem sts each side for shoulders.

FRONT

Work same as back until piece measures 19¾" from beg.

Shape Neck: Bind off center 4 sts and working both sides at once, bind off from each neck edge 2 sts once and 1 st twice. Work even until piece measures 23" from beg. Bind off rem sts each side for shoulders.

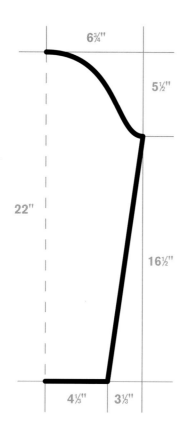

SLEEVES

Cast on 17 sts and work in St st, inc 1 st each side every 7th row once, then every 11th (9th, 9th) row 3 (4, 4) times = 25 (27, 27) sts. Work even until piece measures 16½" from beg.

Shape Cap: Bind off 3 sts at beg of next 2 rows, 2 sts at beg of next 2 rows, dec 1 st each side every 2nd row 4 times, bind off 2 sts at beg of next 2 rows. Bind off rem sts.

FINISHING

Block pieces to finished measurements. Sew shoulder seams. Set in sleeves. Sew side and sleeve seams. With RS facing and crochet hook, work 1 rnd sc evenly around neck edge.

Timeless Tee

■ ■ ■

A classic stands the test of time. The basic tee has certainly done that! It's been a staple of American fashion for decades. This **Workbasket** *1935 tee is revisited in Berroco's simple-to-knit top, richly rendered in Monet yarn.*

■ **PROJECT**
Knit Tee, by Berroco

■ **SKILL LEVEL**
Intermediate

■ **SIZES**
X-Small (Small, Medium, Large, X-Large, XX-Large)
Directions for X-Small with larger sizes in parentheses.
If there is only one figure, it applies to all sizes.

■ **FINISHED MEASUREMENTS**
Bust: 34 (36, 40, 44, 48, 54)"
Length: 21 (21, 21½, 22, 22½, 23)"

■ **MATERIALS**
BERROCO MONET (50 g balls), 9 (10, 11, 12, 13, 14) hanks, Water Lilies. Note: Please see tips on working with Monet before starting to knit. 1 St Marker. Small amt. of smooth yarn in matching color for seaming.

■ **NEEDLES**
Size 10 straight knitting needles OR SIZE TO OBTAIN GAUGE. Size 10 circular knitting needles, 16" length

■ **GAUGE**
7 sts = 2"; 12 rows = 2" in Reverse St st. In order to ensure correct finished measurements, accurate stitch and row gauges must be achieved.
TAKE TIME TO CHECK GAUGE.

1935 Workbasket

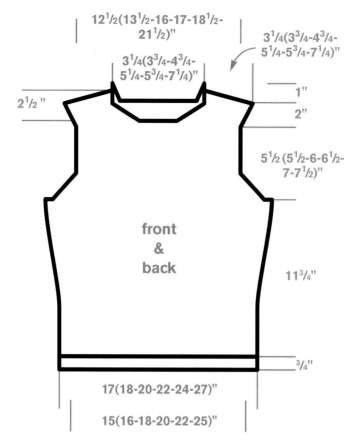

12½(13½-16-17-18½-21½)"

3¼(3¾-4¾-5¼-5¾-7¼)"

3¼(3¾-4¾-5¼-5¾-7¼)"

1"

2½"

2"

5½(5½-6-6½-7-7½)"

front
&
back

11¾"

¾"

17(18-20-22-24-27)"

15(16-18-20-22-25)"

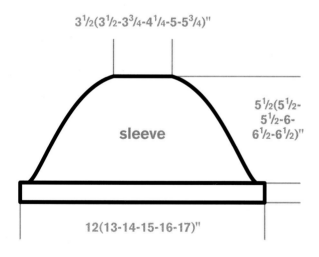

3½(3½-3¾-4¼-5-5¾)"

5½(5½-5½-6-6½-6½)"

sleeve

12(13-14-15-16-17)"

■ TO CHECK GAUGE

Cast on at least 20 sts, using the yarn and needles specified in the instructions. Work pattern for 3". Bind off all sts. Using a ruler as a guide, count the number of sts and rows over 2". (Do not include selvage stitches or cast on and bind off rows.) Divide by 2. If this number is MORE than given in the instructions, try a size larger needle and again check your gauge. If the number is LESS than given in the instructions, try a size smaller and check your gauge. The needle size you use does not matter as long as the stitch and row gauge is accurate.

ABBREVIATIONS

beg = begin(ning); **ch** = chain; **dc** = double crochet; **dec** = decrease; **inc** = increase; **k** = knit; **M1p** = Pickup horizontal strand between st just worked and next st, place on LH needle, p this st (inc 1); **p** = purl; **pat(s)** = pattern(s); **rep** = repeat; **RH** = right hand; **RS** = right side; **rnd(s)** = round(s); **st(s)** = stitch(es); **tog** = together; **WS** = wrong side; **yo** = yarn over; **end on WS** = end having just completed a WS row; **end on RS** = end having just completed a RS row.

GLOSSARY

Stockinette Stitch (St st): K 1 row, p 1 row alternately when working on straight needles. K EVERY round when working on a circular needle.

Garter Stitch: Knit EVERY row when working on

straight needles. K 1 round, p 1 round when working on a circular needle.

Binding Off Across Cables: To dec when binding off across the top of a cable, k2 tog then bind off this st—this counts as 2 sts bound off. This is done to keep the cable from flaring out on the bind-off row and helps keep the shoulders and neck from stretching.

Steam: Lay the piece WS down on a padded surface and cover with a pressing cloth. Press lightly with a steam iron. Set iron down carefully; do not drag as this will stretch the piece. This method will allow you to manipulate fabric and achieve greater length or width, if desired. It will also set stitches and even out the stitch quality for a more professional look.

Steam Lightly: Lay the piece WS down on a padded surface and move steam iron slowly back and forth 1" above piece. Do not allow iron to touch knitted fabric. Steam will allow knitted fabric to blossom. Selvages and ribbings will lay flat. This method may not allow you to block pieces larger or smaller.

TIPS FOR WORKING WITH MONET

1. When working with Monet, it is advisable to keep track of the number of rows worked. This ensures that your back and front will be exactly the same lenth.

2. Keep track of rows and sts when knitting your gauge swatch. Measure your gauge over the entire swatch. Due to the nature of the yarn, it is difficult to count sts and rows.

3. Sew seams with smooth yarn in a similar color.

DIRECTIONS

BACK

With straight needles, cast on 52 (56, 62, 69, 76, 87) sts. Knit 4 rows. Work even in Reverse St st until piece measures 4½" from beg, end on WS. Inc 1 st each end of next row. Rep this inc every 2¼" 3 times more. Work even on 60 (64, 70, 77, 84, 95) sts until piece measures 12½" from beg, end on WS.

Shape Armholes: Bind off 2 sts at beg of the next 2 rows.

Dec Row (RS): P2, P2 tog, p to last 4 sts, p2 tog, p2. Rep this dec every RS row 5 (5, 4, 6, 7, 7) times more. Work even on 44 (48, 56, 59, 64, 75) sts until armholes measure 5½ (5½, 6, 6½, 7, 7½)", end on WS.

Next Row (RS): P2, M1p, p to last 2 sts, M1p, p2. Rep this inc every 1" once more. Work even on 48

(52, 60, 63, 68, 79) sts until armholes measure 7½ (7½, 8, 8½, 9, 9½)", end on WS.

Shape Shoulders and Neck: Next Row (RS): Bind off 3 (5, 5, 6, 6, 9) sts, p until there are 10 (10, 14, 14, 16, 18) sts on RH needle, join another hank of yarn and bind off center 22 (22, 22, 23, 24, 25) sts, p to end. Working both sides at once, bind off 3 (5, 5, 6, 6, 9) sts at beg of the next row, then 4 (4, 6, 6, 7, 8) sts at beg of the next 4 rows. AT THE SAME TIME, dec 1 st at each neck edge EVERY row twice.

FRONT

Work same as for back until armholes measure 5½ (5½, 6, 6½, 7, 7½)", end on WS.

Shape Neck: Next Row (RS): P2, M1p, p until there are 18 (20, 24, 25, 27, 32) sts on RH needle, join another hank of yarn and bind off center 10 (10, 10, 11, 12, 13) sts, p to last 2 sts, M1p, p2. Continue to work incs at each side same as for back and AT THE SAME TIME, bind off 2 sts at each neck edge twice, then dec 1 st at each neck edge every RS row 4 times. When armholes measure 7½ (7½, 8, 8½, 9, 9½)", bind off 3 (5, 5, 6, 6, 9) sts at each armhole edge once, then 4 (4, 6, 6, 7, 8) sts twice for shoulders.

SLEEVES

With straight needles, cast on 42 (46, 49, 53, 56, 60) sts. Knit 4 rows.

Shape Cap: Bind off 2 sts at beg of the next 2 rows.

Dec Row (RS): P2, p2 tog, p to last 4 sts, p2 tog, p2. Rep this dec every RS row 4 (8, 10, 9, 8, 10) times more, then every other RS row 6 (4, 3, 5, 6, 5) times, end on WS. Bind off 2 sts at beg of the next 2 rows. Bind off remaining 12 (12, 13, 15, 18, 20) sts.

FINISHING

Block pieces flat with steam iron and pressing cloth. Sew shoulder seams.

Neckband: With RS facing, using circular needle, beg at center back neck, pick up and k13 (13, 13, 13, 14, 14) sts to left shoulder, 13 sts along left front neck edge, 10 (10, 10, 11, 12, 13) sts across front neck edge, 13 sts along right front neck edge, then 13 (13, 13, 14, 14, 15) sts across remaining back neck edge 62 (62, 62, 64, 66, 68) sts. Mark for beg of rnd and carry marker up. P 1 rnd, k 1 rnd, p 1 rnd. Bind off all sts knitwise. Sew in sleeves. Sew side and sleeve seams.

Divine Duster

■ ■ ■

Svelte, soft and sumptuous, this classic wine duster in Coats & Clark's Red Heart Light & Lofty yarn can rise to most any occasion, formal or casual.

■ **PROJECT**
Light & Lofty Duster, by Coats & Clark

■ **SKILL Level:**
Intermediate

■ **SIZE**
One Size to Fit Bust 36-38"

■ **MATERIALS**
COATS & CLARK RED HEART® "Light & Lofty™" yarn
8 skeins (each skein 6 oz), Wine

■ **NEEDLES**
Size N-15 (10mm) crochet hook or size to obtain guage

■ **GAUGE**
In sc = 8 rows = 4", 8 sts = 4"
TAKE TIME TO CHECK GAUGE.

ABBREVIATIONS

beg = begin(ning); **ch** = chain; **mm** = millimeters; **rem** = remain(ning); **rep** = repeat; **sl** = slip; **sc** = single crochet; **st(s)** = stitch(es); **tog** = together; * = repeat whatever follows the * as indicated.

DIRECTIONS:

BACK

Ch 43. **Row 1:** Sc in 2nd ch from hook and in each ch across; turn—42 sc. **Row 2:** Ch 1, sc in each sc across; turn. Rep Row 2 until 30" from beg.

Shape Raglan: Row 1: Sl st in first sc, sc across next 40 sc; turn (DO NOT WORK LAST SC). **Row 2:** Ch 1, sc in each sc across; turn—40 sc. **Row 3:** Ch 1, sc2tog, sc in each sc across to last 2 sc, sc2tog; turn—38 sc. **Row 4:** Ch 1, sc in each sc across; turn. Rep last 2 rows until 14 sc rem. Fasten off.

RIGHT FRONT

Ch 23. **Row 1:** Sc in 2nd ch from hook and in each ch across; turn—22 sc. **Row 2:** Ch 1, sc in each sc across; turn. Rep Row 2 until 30" from beg.

Shape Raglan: Row 1: Ch 1, sc across 21 sc; turn. **Row 2:** Ch 1, sc in each sc across—21 sc. **Row 3:** Ch 1, sc in each sc across to last 2 sc, sc2tog; turn—20 sc. **Row 4:** Ch 1, sc in each sc across; turn. Rep last 2 rows 6 more times—14sc. **Next Row:** Ch 1, sc 2tog, sc in each sc across to last 2 sc; sc2tog; turn—12 sc. **Next Row:** Ch 1, sc in each sc across; turn—12 sc. Rep last 2 rows until 4 sts rem.

LEFT FRONT

Work same as for Right Front, reverse raglan shaping.

SLEEVES (Make 2)

Ch 21. **Row 1:** Sc in 2nd ch from hook and in each ch across; turn—20 sc. **Row 2:** Ch 1, sc in each sc across; turn. Rep last row until 3" from beg, end wrong side row. Inc 1 sc each end of next row, then every 6th row until 32 sts. Work even in sc 3 more rows.

Shape Raglan: Row 1: Sl 1 st, sc in next 30 sc; turn—30 sc. **Row 2:** Ch 1, sc in each sc across;

turn—30 sc. **Row 3:** Ch 1, sc2tog, sc to last 2 sc, sc2tog; turn—28 sc. **Row 4:** Ch 1, sc in each sc across; turn. Rep last 2 rows until 6 sts rem. Fasten off.

With right sides together, pin raglans in place on front and back pieces of coat and stitch in place.

Border: With right side facing, join yarn at top neck, ch 1, 35 sc across neck and raglan tops; turn. **Row 2:** Ch 1, sc in each sc across—35 sc. **Row 3:** Ch 1, sc in each sc across—DO NOT TURN but turn work and continue working along front edge, sc evenly spaced around working 2 sc in each corner. Fasten off. Sew side and sleeve seams. Weave in ends.

Vintage design.

Artistic License

■ ■ ■

Workbasket's 1966 jacket, inspired by the geometric art of Piet Mondrian, is pure '60s in color! Lion Brand has artfully revived this smart jacket in Cotton Ease yarn, drawing from Mondrian's palette of primary colors. Oh, what a difference color makes!

■ **PROJECT**
Mondrian Cardigan, by Lion Brand

■ **SKILL LEVEL**
Intermediate

■ **SIZES**
Small (Medium, Large, X-Large)
Directions for Small with larger sizes in parentheses.
If there is only one figure, it applies to all sizes.

■ **FINISHED MEASUREMENTS**
Finished chest: 36 (40, 44, 48)"

■ **MATERIALS**
LION BRAND Cotton Ease
A—3 (4, 4, 5) skeins Vanilla
B—1 (1, 2, 2) skeins Licorice
C—1 (1, 1, 1) skein Cherry red

■ **NEEDLES**
Sizes 7 and 8 knitting needles
1 st. holder

■ **BUTTONS**
Seven ¾" buttons of your choice

■ **GAUGE**
With n. 8 needles in stock st 4" square = 17 sts and 22 rows
TAKE TIME TO CHECK GAUGE.

1966 Workbasket

ABBREVIATIONS

beg = begin(ning); **k** = knit; **p** = purl; **RS** = right side; **WS** = wrong side; **dec** = decrease; **sts** = stitches; **beg** = beginning; **ssk** = slip, slip, knit; **sssk** = slip, slip, slip, knit (slip the first, second, and/or third stitch knit-wise one at a time, then insert the tip of left-hand needle into the back of these 2 or 3 sts and knit them together.)

DIRECTIONS

BACK

With B and needle n. 7 cast on 83 (91, 101, 109) sts. Work in seed st as follows: k1, * p1, k 1; for 8 rows. Fasten off B. Join A with needles n. 8 work in stock st until piece measures 14" from start, ending with a p row.

Shape Armholes: Bind off 5 (6, 6, 7) sts at the beg of next 2 rows, dec 1 st each side inside first and last st every 2nd row 4 (4, 6, 6) times; Work dec row as follows: k1, k 2 tog, knit up to last 3 sts, ssk, k1. Work even on 65 (71, 79, 85) sts until armholes measure 7½ (8, 8½, 9)" from beg, ending with a p row.

Shape Shoulders: Bind off 7 (8, 9, 10) sts at beg of next 4 rows, 6 (7, 8, 9) sts at beg of next 2 rows. Leave remaining 25 (25, 27, 27) sts on a st holder for back of neck.

RIGHT FRONT

With needles n. 7 and B cast on 41 (45, 53, 57) sts. Work seed st border as for back. Fasten off B. With A and needles n. 8 work in stock st until 4" above border, and with k row. Fasten off A. With needles n. 7 and B p 1 row. Work in seed st for 7 rows. Fasten off B. With A and needle n. 8 work in stock st until piece measures same length as back to underarm. End with a p row.

Shape Armhole: Work same as right side of back armhole. Work on rem sts for 9 rows counting first armhole row as row 1. End on WS. Fasten off A. With B and needles n. 7 k 1 row. Continue shaping according to directions and only for L and XL sizes, work in seed st for 7 rows. Fasten off B. With C and needles n. 8 work in stock st until 5½ (6, 6, 6½)" above underarm. End with a WS row.

Shape Neckline: (RS)—bind off 7 (7, 8, 8) sts at beg of 1st row, 2 sts at beg of next 2 RS rows. Dec 1 st inside first st every 2nd RS row 3 (3, 4, 4) times. Work on rem 20 (23, 26, 29) sts until armhole measures same as back in length. End with RS row.

Shape Shoulder: Row 1: p and bind off 7 (8, 9, 10) sts at the beg of row, p to end. **Row 2:** knit. **Row 3:** p and bind off 7 (8, 9, 10) sts, p to end. **Row 4:** knit. **Row 5:** p and bind off rem 5 (6, 7, 8) sts. Fasten off last st.

LEFT FRONT

Begin same as right front. Work seed st stripe with B. Fasten off B. With needles n. 8 and C work in stock st until 6" above border. End with a p row. Fasten off C. With B and needles n. 7 k 1 row. Work in seed st for 7 rows. Fasten off B. With needles n. 8 and A work in stock st until same length as back to underarm. End with a p row.

Shape Armhole: Bind off 5 (6, 6, 7) sts, work to end of row. Fasten off A. With needles n. 7 and B p 1 row. Work in seed st for 7 rows, shaping armhole as for back. End on RS. Fasten off B. With needles n. 8 and C p 1 row. Work in stock st and continue shaping armhole for larger sizes for 8 rows, end on RS. Fasten off C. With B and needles n. 7 p 1 row. Work in seed st for 7 more rows, end on RS. Fasten off B. With A and needles n. 8 work in stock st. Shape neckline and shoulder to match right front, but with reverse shaping.

Vintage design.

SLEEVES

With B and needles n. 7 cast on 47 (49, 51, 53) sts. Work in seed st as for back. Fasten off B. With C and needles n. 8 work in stock st for 8 rows. Fasten off C. With B and needles n. 7 k 1 row. Work in seed st for 7 rows. Fasten off B. With A and needles n. 8 work in stock st inc 1 st inside first and last st every 8 rows 8 times 63 (65, 67, 69) sts. Work even until sleeve measures 16" or desired length to underarm.

Sleevecap: Bind off 5 sts at the beg of next 2 rows, dec 1 st each side inside first and last st every 2nd row 14 (15, 16, 17). Dec 2 sts (k 1, k 3 tog—work up to last 4 sts, sssk, k1) every 2nd row twice. Bind off rem 17 sts.

FINISHING AND BORDER

Block pieces to measurements. Sew shoulder seams.

Neck Border: Join B on neck edge of right front. With needles n. 7 pick up and knit 25 (26, 27, 28) sts up to shoulder seam, pick up and knit 25 (25, 27, 27) sts from holder, pick up 25 (26, 27, 28) sts from next shoulder seam to left neck edge. Work on 75 (77, 81, 83) sts in seed st for 8 rows. Next row: (WS) purl and bind off firmly.

Left Front Border: Join B on top edge at corner of neck border. Pick up and knit 84 (86, 88, 90) sts. Work in seed st for 8 rows, bind off with a p row from WS. Place a marker for 7 buttonholes evenly spaced between 3¼" from top and bottom edge, counting 2 sts for each buttonhole.

Right Side Border: In same manner work right side border until 3rd row in seed st is completed. Buttonhole row: Work in pattern. Form 1 buttonhole to correspond to each marker on left edge as follows: Bind off first st, sl last st worked to left needle, k 2 tog. Next row, cast on 2 sts over each buttonhole. Work 3 more rows in seed st, bind off with a purl row on WS.

Sew sides, sew sleeves, set in sleeves. Sew on buttons. Finish off all ends. Steam lightly.

Posh Pullover

■ ■ ■

Workbasket's 1973 Angora-trimmed sweater is lavishly reborn in Berroco's glamorous wide-ribbed pullover in chestnut Chai and luxuriantly trimmed in Zap yarn. The look is faux fur but genuine chic!

■ **PROJECT**
Ribbed Pullover with Fuzzy Collar & Cuffs, by Berroco

■ **SKILL LEVEL**
Beginner

■ **SIZES**
Women's X-Small (Small, Medium, Large, X-Large)
Directions for X-Small with larger sizes in parentheses.
If there is only one figure, it applies to all sizes.

■ **FINISHED MEASUREMENTS**
Bust: 32 (36, 40, 44, 48)"
Length: 21 (21½, 22, 22½, 23)"
Note: This garment is designed to fit closely to the body. There is quite a bit of stretch due to the nature of the ribbing.

■ **MATERIALS**
MC—BERROCO CHAI (50 g), 13 (14, 15, 16, 17) hanks Chestnut
CC—BERROCO ZAP (50 g), 1 (1, 2, 2, 2) hanks Pitch Black
1 St Marker

■ **NEEDLES**
Sizes 8 and 10½ (7 mm) straight knitting needles OR SIZE TO OBTAIN GAUGE.
Size 8 circular knitting needle, 16" length

■ **GAUGE**
14 sts = 4"; 20 rows = 4" in Rib Pat with MC on size 10½ needles. 19 sts = 4"; 27 rows = 4" in St st with CC on size 8 needles.
TAKE TIME TO CHECK GAUGE.

1973 Workbasket

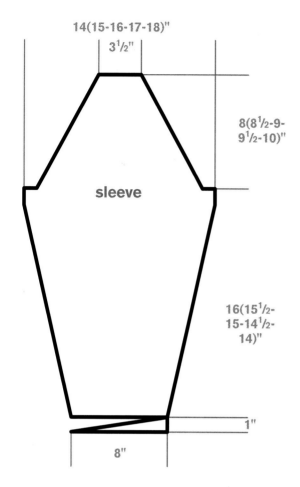

14(15-16-17-18)"

3½"

8(8½-9-9½-10)"

sleeve

16(15½-15-14½-14)"

1"

8"

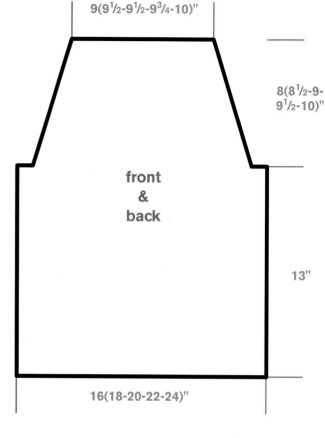

9(9½-9½-9¾-10)"

8(8½-9-9½-10)"

front
&
back

13"

16(18-20-22-24)"

Note: Knit a swatch, steam it, and then take gauge with swatch lying flat, unstretched.

ABBREVIATIONS

beg = beginning; **CC** = contrasting color; **dec** = decrease; **inc** = increase; **k** = knit; **lp(s)** = loop(s); **MC** = main color; **p** = purl; **pat(s)** = pattern(s); **rep** = repeat; **RH** = right hand; **RS** = right side; **rnd(s)** = round(s); **sl** = slip; **SSK** = Sl 2 sts knitwise, insert point of LH needle through FRONTS of these 2 sts and k 2 tog; **st(s)** = stitch(es); **tog** = together; **WS** = wrong side; **yo** = yarn over; **end on WS** = end having just completed a WS row; **end on RS** = end having just completed a RS row.

TIPS FOR WORKING WITH ZAP

1. Cast on and bind off loosely or with larger needles.

2. Take a strand of Zap and pull it through your fingers. Note the directions of the fringe. The strands should flow away from you as you work. Knitting this way will enhance the fullness of Zap garments.

3. From time to time, with the tip of a needle, pull loops formed by Zap ends gently through to release yarn and create greater fullness.

4. Use purl side for RS of work.

DIRECTIONS

RIB PATTERN

Row 1 (RS): K3, * p2, k3, rep from * across.

Row 2: K the k sts and p the p sts as they face you.

Rep these 2 rows for Rib Pat.

BACK

With larger needles, using MC, cast on 58 (63, 73, 78, 83) sts. Work even in Rib Pat until piece measures 13" from beg, end on WS.

Shape Armholes: Bind off 4 sts at beg of the next 2 rows. Work 2 (0, 0, 0, 0) rows even.

Next Row (RS): K2, SSK, work in pat as established to last 4 sts, k2 tog, k2. Keeping 2 sts at each edge in St st, continue to dec in this manner every RS row 0 (0, 8, 11, 14) times more, every other RS row 6 (10, 7, 6, 5) times, then every 6th row 2 (0, 0, 0, 0) times, end on WS. Bind off remaining 32 (33, 33, 34, 35) sts loosely in ribbing.

Vintage design.

FRONT

Work same as for back.

SLEEVES

Note: *Please see previous page for tips for working with Zap before you start to knit.*

With smaller needles, using CC, cast on 38 sts. Work even in Reverse St st for 7 rows, end on RS. Change to larger needles and MC and p the next row, dec 10 sts evenly spaced across—28 sts. Work even in Rib Pat until piece measures 2" from beg, end on WS. Inc 1 st each side of next row. Rep this inc every RS row 0 (0, 0, 1, 6) times more, every 4th row 0 (2, 9, 14, 11) times, every 6th row 8 (9, 4, 0, 0) times, then every 8th row 2 (0, 0, 0, 0) times, working incs into Rib Pat as sts become available. Work even on 50 (52, 56, 60, 64) sts until sleeve measures 17 (16½, 16, 15½, 15)" from beg, end on WS.

Shape Cap: Bind off 4 sts at beg of the next 2 rows.

Next Row (RS): K2, SSK, work in pat as established to last 4 sts, k2 tog, k2. Keeping 2 sts at each edge in St st, continue to dec in this manner every RS row 9 (10, 12, 15, 18) times more, then every other RS row 5 (5, 5, 4, 3) times, end on WS. Bind off remaining 12 sts in ribbing.

FINISHING

Steam pieces to measurements on schematic. Sew raglan sleeve caps to raglan armholes. Sew side and sleeve seams.

Neckband: With RS facing, using circular needle and CC, beg at center back neck, pick up and k16 (16, 16, 17, 17) sts across back neck edge, 12 sts across top of left sleeve, 32 (33, 33, 34, 35) sts across front neck edge, 12 sts across top of right sleeve, then 16 (17, 17, 17, 18) sts across remaining back neck edge—88 (90, 90, 92, 94) sts. Mark for beg of rnd and carry marker up. Purl 7 rnds. Bind off all sts purlwise.

Ravishing in Red

■ ■ ■

Workbasket's *April 1969 crochet shell in marvelous magenta becomes sultry and sophisticated in Tahki Stacy Charles' luscious contemporary version created in sensuous, scarlet Casca yarn.*

■ **PROJECT**
Scarlet Shag Shell, by Tahki Stacy Charles

■ **SKILL LEVEL:**
Beginner

■ **SIZE**
Small

■ **FINISHED MEASUREMENTS**
Finished Chest: 36
Length: 20½"

■ **MATERIALS**
TAHKI STACY CHARLES Austermann Casca Red
5 balls (50g balls)

■ **NEEDLES**
Size 10½ knitting needles
OR SIZE TO OBTAIN GAUGE.

■ **GAUGE**
Gauge 13 sts and 18 rows = 4" over St st.
TAKE TIME TO CHECK GAUGE.

1969 Workbasket

Photo: Courtesy of Tahki Stacy Charles.

ABBREVIATIONS:

beg = Begin(ning); **BO** = bind off; **dec** = decreas(e)(s)(ing); **st(s)** = stitch(es); **rem** = remaining; **St st** = Stockinette stitch; **tog** = together.

DIRECTIONS

BACK

Cast on 57 sts and work in St st until piece meaures 10¼" from beg.

Shape Armholes: Bind off center 3 sts at beg of next 2 rows, then dec 1 st each side every 2nd row 4 times and every 4th row 9 times. Work even until piece measures 19" from beg.

Shape Neckline: Bind off center 9 sts and working both sides at once, bind off from each neck edge 3 sts once, 2 sts once, and 1 st once. Work even until piece measures 20¼" from beg. Bind off rem 2 sts each side for shoulder.

FRONT

Work same as for back until piece measures 17¾" from beg.

Shape Neckline: Bind off center 5 sts and working both sides at once, bind off from each neck edge 2 sts twice and 1 st 4 times.

FINISHING

Block pieces to measurements. Sew shoulders and side seams.

Magnum Opus

■ ■ ■

Workbasket's 1966 cardigan combines casual chic with fashionable function. But Cascade Yarns ups the ante with their contemporary cardigan of Magnum wool in five stunning hues and rich textures . Definitely a magnum opus!

■ **PROJECT**
Multicolor Bulky Cardigan, by Cascade

■ **SKILL LEVEL**
Intermediate

■ **SIZES**
Small (Medium, Large)
Directions for Small with larger sizes in parentheses.
If there is only one figure, it applies to all sizes.

■ **FINISHED MEASUREMENTS**
Finished Chest: $37\frac{1}{2}$ (48, $58\frac{1}{2}$)"

■ **MATERIALS**
CASCADE's Magnum yarn in five colors:
MC A—4 balls brown
MC B—2 balls gray
CC 1—1 ball blue
CC 2—1 ball red
CC 3—1 ball green
14 buttons with shanks

■ **NEEDLES**
Sizes 13 and 15 long circular needles
OR SIZE TO OBTAIN GAUGE

■ **GAUGE**
15 sts and 15 rows equal 10" across and
5" high in pattern using larger needles.
TAKE TIME TO CHECK GAUGE.

1966 Workbasket

ABBREVIATIONS

beg = Begin, beginning; **bet** = between; **BO** = bind off; **CC** = contrasting color; **ch** = chain; **CO** = Cast on; **dc** = double crochet; **dec** = decreas(e)(s)(ing); **eor** = every other row; **inc** = increase(e)(s)(ing); **k** = knit; **lp** = loop; **MC** = main color; **p** = purl; **pat** = pattern; **pm** = place marker; **rem** = remaining; **RS** = right side; **sk** = skip; **st(s)** = stitch(es); **tog** = together; **WS** = wrong side; **yo** = yarn over.

DIRECTIONS

NOTE 1: Garment is made in one piece to underarms.

NOTE 2: Needle size will most greatly effect row gauge and you should obtain at least as many rows per inch that are called for in gauge listed.

NOTE 3: Color sequencing as follows: CC 1, 2, and 3 in that order. MC A & B alternate changing on row 3 after having completed CC 3.

PATTERN STITCH:

Rows 1 and 2: With CC * purl 1, knit 1, purl 1, slip next st holding yarn to back of work * across ending purl 1, knit 1, purl 1.

Rows 3, 4, and 5: With MC * purl 1, knit 1 * across ending purl 1.

BODY

With MC A CO 59 (75, 91) sts.

Row 1: With smaller needles rib row, *k1, p1* across ending K1.

Row 2: *p1, k1* across ending p1. Continue ribbing as set for a total of 4" = 9 rows.

Change to larger needles and CC1 begin pattern st. Work even in pattern for 16 (15, 14)" ODL.

ARMHOLES

Next row divide for armholes by working across 13 (17, 21) sts, BO 1 st, place sts just worked on a holder for right front, work across 31 (39, 47) sts, BO 1 st, place sts just worked on holder for back, work across remaining 13 (17, 21) sts. Work on left front's sts until garment measures 21" from CO edge and a RS row has just been completed.

NECK

BO 3 sts, then 1 eor 2 times. Work even until garment measures 25" from CO edge and shape shoulders by SZ 1 working to 4 sts before armhole edge, wrapping 4th st, turn, work to neck edge, turn working all sts, making sure to pick up wrapped

sts. Place all sts on holder. SZ 2 working to 4 sts before armhole edge. Wrap 4th sts, turn work across, turn, work to 8th st before armhole edge, wrap 8th st. Turn. Work across. Turn. Work across all stitches, picking up wrapped stitches.

Place sts on a holder. SZ 3 work to 5 sts before armhole edge. Wrap 5th st. Turn work to neck edge. Turn work to 10th st before armhole and wrap 10th st. Turn work to neck edge. Turn work to end, picking up all wrapped sts.

Place all sts on holder. Transfer back sts to needle and work in pat as established until garment measures 25" from CO edge. Work across 9 (13, 17) sts, BO center 11 (13, 13) sts, work across to 4 (4, 5) sts before armhole edge. Wrap and turn. BO 1 st at neck edge, turn and work across to 0 (8, 10) sts before armhole. Wrap and turn. Work across to neck edge. Turn work to armhole edge, picking up all wrapped stitches.

Place sts on a holder. Rejoin yarn to neck edge and work to 4 (4, 5) sts before armhole edge. Wrap and turn. BO 1 st at neck edge. Turn and work to 0 (8, 10) sts before armhole edge. Wrap and turn. Work to neck edge, turn, and work across all sts, picking up wrapped sts.

SHOULDERS

Place shoulder sts on a holder. Rejoin yarn at armhole edge of right front and work even until garment measures 21" from CO edge, having just completed a WS row. BO 3 sts, then 1 eor 2 times. Work on remaining sts until garment measures 25" and shape shoulders as before.

Place shoulder sts on holder. Turn garment inside out, and place right front shoulder sts on a needle. Place corresponding back shoulder's sts on another needle. Place these 2 needles parallel with RS of garment facing each other and knit tog 1 st from each needle. Knit tog another st from each needle and pass 1st new st over 2nd. Continue in this manner until all sts are bound off.

Repeat for other shoulder.

RIBBING FRONT AND BOTTOM

Turn garment right side out and with smaller needles and MC A pick up and knit 1 st for every 3 out of 4 rows along left edge, making sure that you have an odd number of sts. Work rib as for bottom boarder for 4" = 9 rows. BO all sts in rib.

BUTTONHOLES

Mark right front edge at 7 different points for buttonholes. The top buttonhole should be about 1/4" from neck edge. Then pick up and knit same num-

Vintage design.

ber of sts with MC A and work as rib, making buttonholes at predetermined places by YO, k2tog on 4th and 8th rows. BO all sts.

SHAWL COLLAR

With right side facing, smaller needles and MC A, pick up and knit 1 st for each bound off st and 3 out of every 4 rows along straight edge of neckhole, making sure there is an odd number of sts. Rib 1 row, then begin shaping shawl collar by short rowing 4 less sts at each edge until center portion meaures 8" and you have worked an equal number of short rows on both sides of collar. Knit across to neckline edge, picking up all wrapped sts. Turn. Work to opposite neck edge, picking up all

wrapped sts. BO all sts in rib.

SLEEVES

With MC A CO 15 (19, 23) sts. With smaller needles rib as set for sweater border for 4". Change to larger needles and CC 1. Work in patt for 17", increasing 1 st at each edge EO 4th row 7 (6, 6) times—29 (31, 35) sts. BO all sts. With matching yarn, sew in sleeve top to armhole opening, leaving edge st unattached. Sew up side seams.

FINISHING

Turn garment inside out and weave in all yarn ends. Sew on buttons to correspond to buttonholes.

Granny Squares Galore!

■ ■ ■

In fashion, everything old is new again. Styles of the '60s and '70s are hot and Granny Squares are climbing the charts! Lion Brand has revised Workbasket's 1975 Granny Squares ensemble with Wool Ease yarn in 10 smashing colors.

■ PROJECT
Granny Squares Cardigan & Shell, by Lion Brand

■ SKILL LEVEL:
Beginner

■ SIZES
Sizes 10 – 12

■ MATERIALS
LION BRAND Wool Ease yarns
Black (2 skeins)
One skein each of the following Wool Ease yarns
(or your choice of colors):

Magenta	Turquoise
Yellow	Orange
Lime	Lilac
Purple	Gray
Coral	Apricot

■ NEEDLES
Size H crochet hook

■ GAUGE
Each square measures approx. 4"
TAKE TIME TO CHECK GAUGE.

1975 Workbasket

cardigan

ABBREVIATIONS

beg = begin(ning); **bet** = between; **BO** = bind off; **CC** = contrasting color; **ch** = chain; **CO** = Cast on; **dc** = double crochet; **dec** = decreas(e)(s)(ing); **eor** = every other row; **hdc** = half double crochet; **inc** = increase(e)(s)(ing); **k** = knit; **lp** = loop; **MC** = main color; **p** = purl; **pat** = pattern; **pm** = place marker; **rnd** = round; **rem** = remaining; **RS** = right side; **sc** = single crochet; **seq** = sequence; **sl st** = slip stitch; **sk** = skip; **sp** = space; **st(s)** = stitch(es); **St st** = Stockinette stitch; **wyif** = with yarn in front; **wyib** = with yarn in back; **WS** = wrong side; **yo** = yarn over.

DIRECTIONS

GRANNY SQUARES

With a CC, ch 4, join with sl st to form ring.

Rnd 1: Ch 3, 2 dc in ring, * ch 1, 3 dc shell in ring, repeat from * twice, ch 1, join in top of ch 3, fasten off.

Rnd 2: Join another CC in any ch 1 sp, ch 3 (counts as 1 dc), (2 dc, ch 1, 3 dc) in same sp, * (3 dc, ch 1, 3 dc) in next ch 1 sp—corner shell made, repeat from * twice, join, fasten off.

Rnd 3: Join a third CC in any corner sp, ch 3, (2 dc, ch 1, 3 dc) in same sp, * 3 dc in sp between corners, (3 dc, ch 1, 3 dc) shell in corner sp, repeat from * twice, 3 dc between shells, join, fasten.

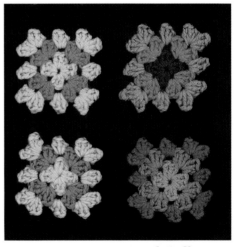

granny square detail

Rnd 4: Join black and any corner sp, ch 3 (2 dc, ch 1, 3 dc) in same sp, * (3 dc in next sp) twice, (3 dc, ch 1, 3 dc) in corner sp, repeat from * twice, 3 dc between each of 2 side shells, join, fasten off.

HALF SQUARES

With a CC, ch 5.

Row 1: (3 dc, ch 1, 3 dc) shell in 5th ch from hook, ch 1, dc in same ch as shell, fasten off, do not turn.

Row 2: Join another CC in third ch of beginning ch, ch 4, 3 dc in first sp, shell in ch 1 sp of shell, 3 dc

shell

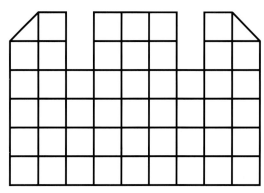

cardigan body
chart I

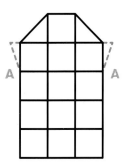

cardigan sleeve
chart II

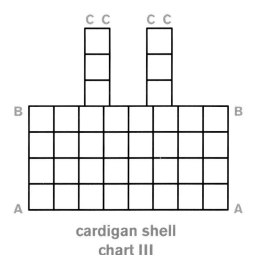

cardigan shell
chart III

in last ch 1 sp, ch 1, dc in dc, fasten off.

Row 3: Join another CC in third ch of ch 4 at beginning of last row, ch 4, 3 dc in each of next 2 sps, shell in shell, 3 dc in each of next 2 sps, ch 1, dc in dc, fasten off.

Row 4: Join black in third ch of ch 4 at beginning of last row, ch 4, 3 dc in each of next 3 sps, shell in shell, 3 dc in each of next 3 sps, ch 1, dc in dc, fasten off.

CARDIGAN

Make 74 squares and 6 half squares, alternating colors as desired on first three rnds.

Front and Back: Sew squares together, following Chart I.

Sleeves: Sew squares together, following Chart II. Work crochet gussets by joining black at A on chart. Sc in each of next 3 sts, hdc in each of next 3 sts, dc to underarm, ch 3, turn. Dc to last 6 dc, hdc in each of next 3 dc, sc in each of last 3 dc, fasten off. Sew shoulder and sleeve seams. Sew sleeves into armholes.

SHELL

Make 38 squares of your choice of varying color combinations. Sew together, following Chart III. Sew seams, back matching As and Bs. This seam will be down middle of back. Then sew sleeve seams CC to back of shell.

FINISHING

Sc around all edges.

Ivory Elegance

Simplicity and elegance are basic ingredients of a classic and this ribbed turtleneck certainly qualifies. The contemporary version is from Cascade's Italian Lana D' Oro line.

■ **PROJECT**
Ivory Turtleneck, by Cascade

■ **SKILL LEVEL**
Beginner

■ **SIZES**
Small (Medium, Large)
Directions for Small with larger sizes in parentheses.
If there is only one figure, it applies to all sizes.

■ **FINISHED MEASUREMENTS**
Finished Bust Size: 46 (49, 52)"

■ **MATERIALS**
CASCADE'S Lana D'Oro Cascade Yarn
Your choice of color, 20 (21, 22) skeins

■ **NEEDLES**
Sizes 3 and 6 knitting needles

■ **GAUGE**
Tension: Using #6 needle and in rib pattern slightly stretched, 8 sts = 1"
TAKE TIME TO CHECK GUAGE.

ABBREVIATIONS

beg = begin(ning); **ch** = chain; **dc** = double crochet; **rep** = repeat(s); **rev** = revers(e)(ing); **st(s)** = stitch(es); **t-ch** = turning chain; **WS** = wrong side

DIRECTIONS

BACK

With #3 needle cast on 182 (198, 208) sts and work in knit 2, purl 2 rib ending the row with knit 2 for 17 (18, 19)".

Shape Armholes: Keeping pattern correct, bind off 3 sts at the beginning of the next 2 rows, then 1 st at the beginning of the next 2 rows, then 1 st at the beginning of the next 2 rows. 170 (186, 196) sts remaining. Continue straight until armhole measures 10".

Shape Back, Neck, and Shoulders: Keeping pattern correct, bind off 24 (28, 31) sts, pattern 24 (28, 30) sts, turn and leave remaining sts on hold for later. Work 1 row back, turn, bind off 24 (28, 30) sts Rejoin yarn and bind off the center 74 sts loosely and pattern to end. Bind off 24 (28, 31) sts pattern to end. Turn and work to end. Bind off remaining 24 (28, 30) sts.

FRONT

Work as for back until piece measures 6½" above armhole shaping.

Shape Front Neck and Shoulders: Pattern 75 (83, 88) sts, turn and work back, leaving remaining sts on hold for later. Working on left front only, *at neck edge only*, bind off 8 sts 1 time, 4 sts 2 times, 3 sts 1 time, 2 sts 1 time and 1 st 6 times. 48 (56, 61) sts remaining. When armhole measures 10" shape shoulders as follows: on outside edge only, bind off 24 (28, 31) sts. Pattern to end, turn and pattern back. Bind off remaining sts. Rejoin yarn and bind off center 20 sts and pattern to end. Work right shoulder as for left side.

SLEEVES

With #3 needles cast on 86 sts and work in k2, p2 rib as for back for 2". Change to #6 needles and continue until sleeve measures 4". Start increases: continuing in rib pattern increase 1 st at each edge on this row and every following 3rd row to 164 sts. When sleeve measures 24", shape sleeve top. Bind off 12 sts at the beginning of the next 2 rows, then 9 sts at the beginning of the next 8 rows. Bind off 14 sts at the beginning of the next 2 rows, then bind off remaining 40 sts.

Photo: Courtesy of Cascade Yarns.

COLLAR

Collar is worked alone and sewn on sideways. With #3 needle, cast on 86 sts and work in k2, p2 rib for 25" and bind off. Sew together bind off and cast on edges. Sew collar to neck of sweater with the seam facing the outside. Sew shoulder seams and side seams. Set in sleeves. Roll back a 4" cuff.

Crimson Tide

■ ■ ■

The waves of fashion are sometimes fleeting, but tropical is always in! Try this simple, loosely knit pullover by Tahki Stacy Charles, done in red-hot Austermann Zoom yarn. But cool as a sea breeze!

■ **PROJECT**
Loose-Knit Red Pullover, by Tahki Stacy Charles

■ **SKILL LEVEL**
Beginner

■ **SIZE**
Small

■ **MATERIALS**
TAHKI STACY CHARLES Austermann Zoom
4 balls (each ball is 100 grams) Red #3.
Stitch Holder
Pink Ribbon to match yarn (1 yd or more, if desired)

■ **NEEDLES**
Size 15mm knitting needles
Size 12mm crochet hook

■ **GAUGE**
7, 25 sts and 12 rows = 4" over lace pat.
TAKE TIME TO CHECK GAUGE.

Photo: Courtesy of Tahki Stacy Charles.

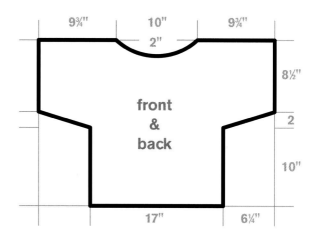

9¾" 10" 9¾"

2"

8½"

front
&
back

2

10"

17" 6¼"

Workbasket magazine often featured celebrities as models or as needlecraft designers. Here, movie and theater actress, Anne Bobby, ("Born on the Fourth of July," "Burden of Proof") models a crocheted sweater featured in *Workbasket's* April 1992 issue. Anne is also an accomplished needle artist whose works have appeared in the Metropolitan Museum of Modern Art.

ABBREVIATIONS

Beg = Begin(ning); **bet** = between; **BO** = bind off; **CC** = contrasting color; **ch** = chain; **CO** = cast on; **dc** = double crochet; **dec** = decreas(e)(s)(ing); **eor** = every other row; **inc** = increase(e)(s)(ing); **k** = knit; **lp** = loop; **MC** = main color; **p** = purl; **pat** = pattern; **pm** = place marker; **rem** = remaining; **RS** = right side; **sc** = single crochet; **seq** = sequence; **sk** = skip; **ssk** = slip, slip, knit; **sssk** = slip, slip, slip, knit (slip the first, second, and/or third stitch knitwise one at a time, then insert the tip of left-hand needle into the back of these 2 or 3 sts and knit them together); **st(s)** = stitch(es); **St st** = Stockinette stitch; **tog** = together; **wyif** = with yarn in front; **wyib** = with yarn in back; **WS** = wrong side; **yo** = yarn over.

DIRECTIONS

LACE PATTERN

Worked over a multiple of 4 sts + 2 selvage sts.

Row 1: 1 selvage st, P2, * yo, P4 tog; rep from *, end P2, 1 slevage st.

Row 2: 1 selvage st, K2, * K1, in next yo work K1, P1 and K1; rep from *, end K2, 1 selvage st.

Row 3: 1 selvage st, P1, *yo, P4 tog; rep from *, end P3, 1 selvage st.

Row 4: 1 selvage st, K3, *K1, in next yo work K1, P1 and K1; rep from *, end K1, 1 selvage st.

Rep rows 1-4 for lace pat.

BACK

Cast on 34 sts and work in garter st for 2 rows. Work in lace pat for 10".

SLEEVES

Cast on 4 sts at beg of next 6 rows = 58 sts. Work 6½" more. Work even until piece measures 18½" from beg.

NECK

Shape Neck: Bind off center 12 sts and working both sides at once, bind off from each neck edge 3 sts once. Work even until piece measures 20½" from beg. Place remaining 20 sts on a holder.

FRONT

Work same as back.

FINISHING

Block pieces to measurements. Weave (or k) shoulders tog. Sew side seams. For neckband, with RS facing and crochet hook, work 1 rnd sc (54 sts) and 1 rnd backwards sc (from left to right) evenly around neck edge. Work in same way around lower edge of sleeves (working 22 sts). Weave ribbon through neck and tie at center front.

With All the Trimmings!

This fluff-trimmed cardigan from the 1960s becomes sumptuous and seductive in Berroco's glorious Optik yarn trimmed with Zap and sparkling paillettes of Lazer FX.

■ **PROJECT**
Button-front Cardigan with Fluff Collar & Cuffs, by Berroco

■ **SKILL LEVEL**
Intermediate

■ **SIZES**
Women's X-Small (Small, Medium, Large, X-Large, XX-Large)
Directions for X-Small with larger sizes in parentheses.
If there is only one figure, it applies to all sizes.

■ **FINISHED MEASUREMENTS**
Bust (butttoned): 36 (38, 40, 42, 44, 46)"
Length: 22 (22½, 23, 23½, 24, 24½)"

■ **MATERIALS**
A—BERROCO OPTIK (50 g) 9 (9, 10, 10, 11, 11) hanks Van Gogh
B—BERROCO LAZER FX (10 g) 3 (3, 3, 3, 3, 4) balls Gold/Black
C—Optional: BERROCO ZAP (50 g), 1 hank Olive
Seven ¾" buttons

■ **NEEDLES**
Sizes 7 or 8 straight knitting needles
OR SIZE TO OBTAIN GAUGE.
Size 6 mm (J) crochet hook for Zap trim.

■ **GAUGE**
16 sts = 4"; 24 rows = 4" in St st on size 8 needles
TAKE TIME TO CHECK GAUGE.

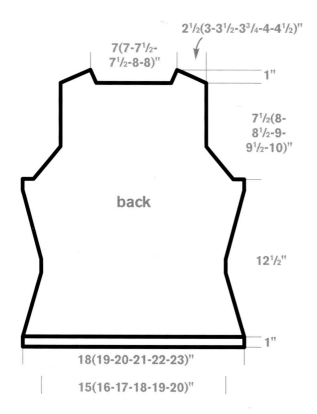

2½(3-3½-3¾-4-4½)"

7(7-7½-7½-8-8)"

1"

7½(8-8½-9-9½-10)"

back

12½"

1"

18(19-20-21-22-23)"

15(16-17-18-19-20)"

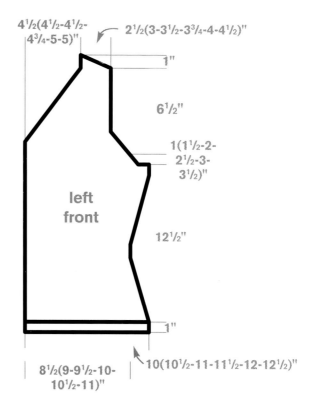

4½(4½-4½-4¾-5-5)"

2½(3-3½-3¾-4-4½)"

1"

6½"

1(1½-2-2½-3-3½)"

left front

12½"

1"

8½(9-9½-10-10½-11)"

10(10½-11-11½-12-12½)"

ABBREVIATIONS

beg = begin(ning); **CC** = contrasting color; **ch** = chain; **dc** = double crochet; **dec** = decrease; **inc** = increase; **k** = knit; **KSP** = K1, then sl st back to LH needle, lift 2nd st on LH needle back over returned st and replace returned st on RH needle (1 st dec'd); **K2SP** = K2 tog, then sl st back to LH needle, lift 2nd st on LH needle back over returned st and replace returned st on RH needle (2 sts dec'd); **lp(s)** = loop(s); **MC** = main color; **M1k** = pickup horizontal strand between st just worked and next st, place on LH needle, k this st (inc 1); **M1p** = pickup horizontal strand between st just worked and next st, place on LH needle, p this st (inc 1); **p** = purl; **psso** = pass sl st over k st; **pat(s)** = pattern(s); **rep** = repeat; **RH** = right hand; **RS** = right side; **rnd(s)** = round(s); **sc** = single crochet; **SKP** = sl 1, k 1, psso; **sl** = slip; **SSK** = Sl 2 sts knitwise, insert point of LH needle through FRONTS of these 2 sts and k 2 tog; **st(s)** = stitch(es); **TBL** = through back lp(s); **tog** = together; **WS** = wrong side; **wyib** = with yarn in back; **wyif** = with yarn in front; **yo** = yarn over; **end on WS** = end having just completed a WS row; **end on RS** = end having just completed a RS row.

TIPS FOR WORKING WITH (optional) ZAP

1. Cast on and bind off loosely or with larger needles.

2. Take a strand of Zap and pull it through your fingers. Note the directions of the fringe. The strands should flow away from you as you work. Knitting this way will enhance the fullness of Zap garments.

3. From time to time, with tip of needle, pull loops formed by Zap ends gently through to release yarn and create greater fullness.

4. Use purl side for RS of work.

DIRECTIONS

NOTE 1: After ribbing has been completed, B should be added to A every 5th row. Work with both yarns held tog on that row.

NOTE 2: When B is not in use, it may be carried loosely up the side of work, making sure to wrap both yarns tog every other row to eliminate long loops.

BACK

With smaller needle, using A, cast on 73 (77, 81, 85, 89, 93) sts.

Row 1 (RS): K1, * pl, k1, rep from * across.

Row 2: P1, * k1, p1, rep from * across. Rep these 2 rows until piece measures 1" from beg, end on WS, dec 1 st at end of last row—72 (76, 80, 84, 88, 92) sts. Change to larger needles and work in St st, adding B as in note, dec 1 st each side every ¾" 4 times, then every 1" twice—60 (64, 68, 72, 76, 80) sts. Work even until piece measures 7" from beg, end on WS. Inc 1 st each end of next row, then every 1" 5 times more—72 (76, 80, 84, 88, 92) sts. Work even

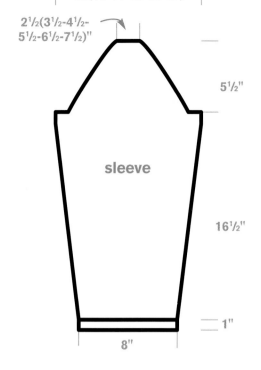

12(13-14-15-16-17)"

2½(3½-4½-
5½-6½-7½)"

5½"

sleeve

16½"

1"

8"

---

until piece measures 13½" from beg, end on WS.

Shape Armholes: Bind off 4 sts at beg of the next 2 rows. Dec 1 each side every RS row 8 times—48 (52, 56, 60, 64, 68) sts. Work even until armholes measures 7½ (8, 8½, 9, 9½, 10)", end on WS.

Shape Shoulders and Neck: Next Row (RS): Bind off 4 (4, 5, 5, 6, 6) sts, k until there are 7 (9, 9, 11, 11, 13) sts on RH needle, join another hank of A and bind off center 26 (26, 28, 28, 30, 30) sts, k to end. Working both sides at once, bind off 4 (4, 5, 5, 6, 6) sts at beg of the next row, then 3 (4, 4, 5, 5, 6) sts at beg of the next 4 rows. AT THE SAME TIME, dec 1 st at each neck edge every RS row once.

LEFT FRONT

With smaller needle, using A, cast on 41 (43, 45, 47, 49, 51) sts.

Row 1 (RS): K1, * p1, k1, rep from * to last 2 sts, end k2.

Row 2: K2, p1, * k1, p1, rep from * across. Rep these 2 rows until piece measures 1" from beg, end on WS, dec 1 st at end of last row— 40 (42, 44, 46, 48, 50) sts. Change to larger needles. Keeping 2 sts at front edge in Garter St and remaining sts in St st, add B as in note. Dec 1 st at armhole edge every ¾" 4 times, then every 1" twice—34 (36, 38, 40, 42, 44) sts. Work even until piece measures 7" from beg, end on WS. Inc 1 st at beg of the next row, then every 1" 5 times

more—40 (42, 44, 46, 48, 50) sts. Work even until piece measures 13½" from beg, end on WS.

Shape Armholes: Bind off 4 sts at beg of the next row. Dec 1 st at armhole edge every RS row 8 times. AT THE SAME TIME, when armhole measures 1½", end on WS.

Shape V-Neck: New Row (RS): Continuing to shape armhole, work to last 4 sts, k2tog, k2. Rep this dec every RS row 15 (14, 14, 12, 13, 12) times more, then every other RS row 2 (3, 4, 6, 6, 7) times—10 (12, 13, 15, 16, 18) sts. When armhole measures 7½ (8 , 8½, 9, 9½, 10)", end on WS. Bind off 4 (4, 5, 5, 6, 6) sts at armhole edge once, then 3 (4, 4, 5, 5, 6) sts twice for shoulder. Mark the position of 7 buttons evenly spaced along front edge, with the first at top of ribbing, the last ½" below start of neck shaping and the other 5 spaced evenly between.

RIGHT FRONT

Work to correspond to left front, reversing all shaping and working next decs as k2, SSK. Make buttonholes on RS rows opposite markers as k2, k2 tog, yo, k to end.

SLEEVES

With smaller needles, using A, cast on 33 sts. Work in ribbing same as for back for 1", end on WS, dec 1 st at end of last row—32 sts. Change to larger needles and work in St st, adding B as in note, inc 1 st each side every 4th row 0 (0, 0, 0, 1, 7) times, every 6th row 0 (0, 1, 9, 15, 11) times, then every 8th row 0 (3, 11, 5, 0, 0) times, then every 10th row 1 (7, 0, 0, 0, 0) times, then every 12th row 7 (0, 0, 0, 0, 0) times—48 (52, 56, 60, 64, 68) sts. Work even until sleeve measures 17½" from beg, end on WS.

Shape Cap: Bind off 4 sts at beg of the next 2 rows. Dec 1 st each side every RS row 13 times, then every other RS row twice. Bind off remaining 10 (14, 18, 22, 26, 30) sts.

FINISHING

Sew shoulder seams. Sew in sleeves. Sew side and sleeve seams.

Neck Edging (Optional): With RS facing, using crochet hook and C, beg at right front edge, work 1 row sc around entire neck edge. Fasten off. Rejoin yarn in first sc and, with RS facing, work 1 sc in each sc around. Fasten off.

Sleeve Edging (Optional): With RS facing, using crochet hook and C, beg at sleeve seam, work 1 rnd sc around lower edge of sleeve, join with sl st in first sc. Ch1, then work 1 sc in each sc around, join with sl st in first sc. Fasten off. Sew on buttons.

Needlework Nouveau

■ ■ ■

Tatting is making a comeback in the most unlikely places—in teen fashions as chokers, earrings, and even belts! But you don't have to be a teen to wear this tasteful beaded ensemble by Handy Hands, inspired from a 1954 Workbasket *issue.*

■ PROJECT
Tatted Choker & Earrings, by Handy Hands

■ SKILL LEVEL
Beginner

■ MATERIALS
Flora Size 10 thread, color of your choice
Approx. 30 seed beads for 12" choker, 9 each for earrings
Pierced earring wires

■ NEEDLES
Shuttle or tatting needle

ABBREVIATIONS
Rw = Row; **Ch** = Chain(s); **Cl** = Close ring.

CHOKER DIRECTIONS

Note: See How-To Tat Basics beginning on page 120 for more information and Diagrams.

To do a +b, slide a bead on a small crochet hook, hook the picot, slide the bead on the picot and join as normal.

Pre-string 30 beads. (You may want to string more if you want the choker longer. Figure 2½. beads per inch.)

1954 Workbasket

Ch 1-3-4-4-4-4 +b (join to first picot of this chain). Rw.

Ch 4-4-4-4-4-4 +b (join to first picot of this chain). Rw

Repeat from * to * for desired length.

Join to the beginning. Tie/Hide/Cut.

FOR END TIES: Thread 12" length of thread through each picot end of choker so there are two 6" lengths and knot securely. Tie small bow or loose knot at nape of the neck to secure.

EARRINGS DIRECTIONS

Pre-string 9 beads for each earring.

Ch 1-1 Rw.

Ch 6-2 Rw.

Ch +b (to 1st picot made) 6-2 Rw.

Ch +b (to 2nd picot made) 8-2 Rw.

Ch +b (to 3rd picot made) 8-2 Rw.

Ch +b (to 4th picot made) 10-2 Rw.

Ch +b (to 5th picot made) 10-2 Rw.

Ch +b (to 6th picot made) 8-2 Rw.

Ch +b (to 7th picot made) 8, pull up bead for picot, 2 Rw.

Ch +b (to 8th picot made) 1. Tie/Hide/Cut.

Thread pierced earring wires on each smaller picot end.

Town & Country Cardigan

∎ ∎ ∎

*When it comes to style **and** practicality, button-front cardigans make all kinds of horse sense. This beautiful textured sweater with wooden buttons designed by Coats & Clark is rendered in rustic Red Heart Tweed. Perfect for a walk—**or ride**—in the country!*

■ **PROJECT**
Tweed Cardigan, by Coats & Clark

■ **SKILL LEVEL**
Intermediate

■ **SIZES**
Small (Medium, Large, X-Large)
Directions for Small with larger sizes in parentheses.
If there is only one figure, it applies to all sizes.

■ **MATERIALS**
COATS & CLARK Red Heart® "Tweed™" yarn
8 (9, 10, 10) skeins Cranberry
Five ¾" buttons

■ **NEEDLES**
Size F and H crochet hook
Yarn needle
Sewing needle
Thread to match

■ **GAUGE**
16 sts and 13 rows = 4" in pattern st using size H needle
18 sts and 20 rows = 4" in sc using size F needle
TAKE TIME TO CHECK GAUGE.

ABBREVIATIONS

beg = begin(ning); **ch** = chain; **dc =** double crochet; **dec =** decrease; **ea** = each; **est** = established; **mm** = millimeters; **pat** = pattern; **rem** = remain(ning); **rep** = repeat; **sl** = slip; **sc** = single crochet; **st(s)** = stitch(es); **tog** = together; * = repeat whatever follows the * as indicated: **yo** = yarn over.

PATTERN STITCH

Note: (Multiple of 3 plus 2).

Base row: (Right side) ch3 (counts as 1 dc), 1 dc in the 2nd st, 1 dc in ea st across.

Row 1: ch1, 1 sc into ea st across, 1 sc into the top of the turning ch.

Row 2: ch3, 1dc into the 2nd st. * tr/rf of dc below next st, skip 1 st, 1dc into ea of the next 2 sts, repeat from * across.

DIRECTIONS

RIBBING

Using size F needle, ch 13.

Row 1: 1 sc into the 2nd from needle, 1 sc into the next 11 ch, turn.

Row 2: Ch 1, 1 sc into the back of ea st across, turn. Repeat row 2 and work until ribbing measures 17½ (19½, 20½, 21½)".

Using size H needle (right side) work 74 (83, 86, 92) dc along long edge of ribbing. Work in pattern st beginning with row 1 until back measures 23½ (24½, 25, 26)" ending with a wrong side row. Fasten off.

POCKET LININGS (Make 2)

Using size H needle ch 20.

Row 1: 1 dc into the 3rd ch from needle and ea of the next 16 chs, turn.

Row 2: Ch 1, 1sc into ea st across, 1 sc into the top of the turning ch, turn.

Row 3: Ch 3, 1 dc into the 2nd st, 1 dc into ea st acorss, turn. Repeat rows 2 and 3 until pocket lining measures 4" ending with row 1. Fasten off.

LEFT FRONT

Using size F needle, work ribbing same as for back to 8¾ (9¾, 10¼, 10¾)". Using size H needle, work 35 (41, 41, 44) dc along long edge of ribbing. Work in pattern until front measures 6½" ending with a wrong side row. Next work 8 (11, 11, 12) sts in est pattern, continuing in est pattern work 17 sts across top of pocket lining, work 10 (13, 13, 15) st in patt. Continue to work in est pattern until front measures 14 (14½, 14½, 15)" ending with a wrong side row.

NECK SHAPING

Work in est patt to the last 2 sts, dc2tog (dec made). Dec 1 st at neck edge every right side row 7 (7, 7, 8) times more, then dec 1 st at neck edge every 2nd right side row 1 (2, 2, 2) times. Work even on 26 (31, 31, 33) sts until front measures 23½ (24½, 25, 26)" with a wrong side row. Fasten off.

RIGHT FRONT

Work the same as right front to 6½". Next row: Work 10 (13, 13, 15) sts, work 17 sts across top of pocket lining, work 8 (11, 11, 12) sts.

Work the same as right front to neck shaping.

NECK SHAPING

Ch2, yo and draw up a loop in the 2nd st, yo, draw thru 2 loops, yo, draw thru 3 loops (dec made), work in est pattern to end of row.

Finish same as right front having neck increases at beg of row.

SLEEVES

Work ribbing same as for back to 7½ (7½, 8, 8)". Using size H needle work 41 (41, 44, 47) dc along long edge of ribbing. Work in pattern and inc 1 st ea end of the row every right side row 14 (16, 16, 17) times, then every 2nd right side row 4 times. Work even on 77 (81, 84, 89) sts until sleeve measures 17½ (18, 18½, 19)" ending with a wrong side row. Fasten off.

FINISHING

Sew pocket lining to inside of fronts. Using size H needle work 1 sc into ea st across the 17 sts of pocket opening, ch 1, work 1 reverse sc into ea st across. Fasten off.

Sew Shoulder Seams: Place a marker 9½ (10, 10½, 11)" below shoulder seam on front and back. Sew sleeve between markers. Sew side and sleeve seams.

Weave in all yarn ends.

FRONT AND NECK BAND

Row 1: With right side facing using size F needle, work 106 (110, 112, 117) sc sts along right front edge, work 1 sc into ea st across back neck, work 106 (110, 112, 117) sc sts along left front edge, turn.

Row 2: Ch1, 1 sc into ea st around, turn.

Row 3: Mark 5 buttonholes evenly spaced, the top buttonhole 3 sts below the first neck dec and the bottom buttonhole 3 sts above bottom edge. Ch1 [1 sc into ea st to marker, ch3, skip 3 sc sts] 5 times, 1 sc into ea st to end of row, turn.

Row 4: [1 sc into ea st to the ch3, 1 sc into ea of the 3 ch sts] 5 times, 1 sc into ea st to the end of row, turn.

Row 5: Ch1, 1 sc into each st to end. Finish off.

Coats & Clark's Red Heart® Tweed™ yarns come in numerous colors rich in variegated hues such as cranberry, shown above, used in this featured cardigan.

Chenille Meets Chanel

■ ■ ■

This striped pullover in a 1964 Workbasket
*issue sports classic Chanel flair. Coats & Clark's similar
version adds a little twist
to the texture with their rich chenille-feel
Baby Teri yarn, soft and subtle in pink and white.*

■ PROJECT
Powder Puff Sweater, by Coats & Clark

■ SKILL LEVEL
Beginner

■ SIZES
Small (Medium, Large)
Directions for Small with larger sizes in parentheses.
If there is only one figure, it applies to all sizes.

■ FINISHED MEASUREMENTS
To Fit Chest: 32 (36, 40)"
Finished Chest Measurement: 40 (44, 48)"

■ MATERIALS
COATS & CLARK Red Heart Baby Teri®
3-Ply Light Worsted-Weight Yarn (3 oz. skeins)
CA—7 (8, 8) skeins, White
CB—6 (7, 7) skeins, Pink

■ NEEDLES
Size I-9 and K-10.5 SUSAN BATES® crochet hooks
OR SIZE TO OBTAIN GAUGE

■ GAUGE
22 sts = 9", 25 rows = 12" with larger hook
TAKE TIME TO CHECK GAUGE.

1964 Workbasket

ABBREVIATIONS

beg = begin(ning); **bpdc** = back post double crochet; **ch** = chain; **cont** = continue; **dc** = double crochet; **dec** = decrease; **est** = established; **fpdc** = front post double crochet; **hdc** = half double crochet; **lp** = loop; **pat** = pattern; **rem** = remaining; **rep** = repeat; **sk** = skip; **sp** = space; **st(s)** = stitch(es); **sc** = single crochet; **RS** = right side; **WS** = wrong side; * = repeat whatever follows the * as indicated; **yo** = yarn over.

Note: Entire sweater is worked holding 2 strands together. Change colors every 4 rows.

Back & Front Color Sequence: CA & CB, CB & CB, CA & CB, CA & CA.

Sleeve Color Sequence: CA & CA, CA & CB, CB & CB, CA & CB.

DIRECTIONS

BACK

With larger hook using CA & CB ch 50 (56, 60).

Work (sc, dc) in 2nd ch from hook, * sk next ch, (sc, dc) in next ch, rep from * to last 2 ch, sk next ch, sc in last ch; turn—49 (55, 59) st.

Pat Row: Ch 1, * (sc, dc) in sc, sk dc, rep from * to last st, sc in last sc; turn.

Following color sequence rep pat row 22½ (23½, 24½)" from beg.

SHAPE SHOULDERS

Work pat row for 17 (19, 21) st. Fasten off. Skip next 15 (17, 17) st. Attach yarn in next st, ch 1, work pat row across. Fasten off.

FRONT

Work same as back until 6 rows less than back.

FIRST SHOULDER SHAPING

Rep pat row for 21 (23, 25) sts; turn. Cont rep Pat Row, following color sequence until front is same length as back, at the same time, dec 2 st at next edge on next 2 rows. Fasten off.

SECOND SHOULDER SHAPING

Sk next 7 (9, 9) st.

Rep as for First Shoulder.

SLEEVES

Put mark 10 (11, 12)" down from shoulder on front and back. With RS facing, using larger hook, attach CA & CA at mark. Ch 1, work (sc, dc) 24 (27, 29) times evenly spaced between markers, work sc; turn—49 (55, 59) sts.

Following color sequence, work 2 pat rows then 1 dec row 10 (10, 9) times, then work dec row till 27 (29, 29) st rem. Fasten off.

Dec Row: Ch 1, * (sc, dc) in sc, sk dc, rep from * to last 7 st, sc in next sc, yo insert hook in same st as last sc, yo, draw loop through, sk next dc, insert hook in next sc, yo, draw loop through, yo, draw loop through 3 loops on hook, yo, draw through 2 loops on hook, insert hook in last sc used, yo, draw loop through, sk next dc, insert hook in next sc, yo, draw loop through, yo, draw loop through 3 loops on hook, dc in last sc used, sk next dc, sc in last sc; turn—2 st dec.

Sew side and sleeve seams.

SLEEVE & BOTTOM RIBBING

Rnd 1: With RS facing, attach CA & CA at opening, with smaller hook ch 2 (counts as 1 hdc), work an even number of hdc evenly spaced around opening, join in top of beg ch 2.

Rnd 2: Ch 2, * fpdc around post of next st, bpdc around post of next st, rep from * to last st, fpdc around post of last st, join in top of beg ch 2.

Rep Rnd 2 until ribbing is 2". Fasten off.

The powder puff-soft baby Teri yarn, made by Coats & Clark Red Heart, has a unique chenille-like texture and comes in many colors.

NECK RIBBING

With RS facing, attach CA & CA at neck, with smaller hook ch 2 (counts as 1 hdc), work an even number of hdc evenly spaced around neck opening, join in top of beg ch 2. Rep Rnd 2 of sleeve & bottom ribbing for 1½". Fasten off.

Love Triangle

■ ■ ■

*Fashion has rekindled its love affair with shawls. And why not! They combine Old World romance **and** contemporary casual elegance. This triangle shawl by Lion Brand—reminiscent of one in a 1973* **Workbasket** *issue—is done in glorious lilac Wool Ease. No cold shoulders here!*

■ **PROJECT**
Fringed Triangular Shawl, by Lion Brand

■ **SKILL LEVEL**
Intermediate

■ **SIZES**
One size fits all.

■ **FINISHED MEASUREMENTS**
60" across at widest point

■ **MATERIALS**
LION BRAND Wool-Ease® 4 balls (5 oz/435 yd)
Lilac or color of your choice

■ **NEEDLES**
Size H-8 (5 mm) crochet hook
or size to obtain gauge

■ **GAUGE**
18 sts + 8 rows = 4" in pattern.
TAKE TIME TO CHECK GAUGE.

ABBREVIATIONS

beg = begin(ning); **ch** = chain; **dc** = double crochet;
rep = repeat(s); **rev** = revers(e)(ing); **st(s)** =
stitch(es); **t-ch** = turning chain; **WS** = wrong side.

1973 Workbasket

DIRECTIONS

Row 1: Ch 4, 2 dc in 4th ch from hook—counts as 3 dc.

Row 2: Ch 3 (counts as 1 dc now and each row hereafter), turn. 2 dc in first dc, ch 1, skip 1 dc, 3 dc in 3rd ch of beg-ch of row 1 – 6 dc.

Row 3: Ch 3, turn. 2 dc in first dc, ch 2, dc in ch1-space, ch 2, 3 dc in top of t-ch—7 dc.

Row 4: Ch 3, turn. 2 dc in first dc, ch 1, skip 1 dc, 3 dc in next dc, ch 1, skip (ch 2, dc, ch 2), 3 dc in next dc, ch 1, skip 1 dc, 3 dc in top of t-ch— 12 dc.

Row 5: Ch 3, turn. 2 dc in first dc, ch 2, skip 2 dc, 1 dc in ch1-space, ch 2, skip 3 dc, 3 dc in ch1-space, ch 2, skip 3 dc, 1 dc in ch1-space, ch 2, skip 2 dc, 3 dc in top of t-ch—11 dc.

Row 6: Ch 3, turn. 2 dc in first dc, ch 1, skip 1 dc, 3 dc in next dc, * ch1, skip (ch 2, dc, ch 2), 3 dc in next dc, ch 1, skip 1 dc, 3 dc in next dc; rep from *, end last rep 3 dc in top of t-ch.

Row 7: Ch 3, turn. 2 dc in first dc, ch 2, skip 2 dc, * 1 dc in ch1-space, ch 2, skip 3 dc, 3 dc in ch1-space, ch 2, skip 3 dc; rep from *, end last rep dc in ch1-space, ch 2, skip 2 dc, 3 dc in top of t-ch.

Repeat Rows 6 and 7 until shawl measures 60" across, end with Row 6.

Final Row: Ch 3, turn, 1 dc in first dc, ch 1, skip 2 dc, *1 dc in ch1-space, ch 1, skip 3 dc, 3dc in ch1-space, ch 1, skip 3 dc; rep from *, end, 1 dc in ch1-space, ch 1, sk 2 dc, 2 dc in top of t-ch. Work 1 row single crochet evenly across top edge. Fasten off.

FRINGE

Cut strands 16" long. With WS of shawl facing, fold 4 strands in half and draw loops through lowest corner with hook, pull ends through loops and pull knot tight; rep at ends of every other row along short sides of shawl, with last fringe at corner.

Winter Woolies

Workbasket's *1970 scarf and fluff-top snowcap are cute, but Berroco's contemporary version in hot Hip Hop yarn sports cache with flair and flashy fringe. And, good news—this set is super easy to make!*

■ **PROJECT**
Fringed Scarf, Cap, & Mittens, by Berroco

■ **SKILL LEVEL**
Very Easy

■ **SIZE**
One size fits all

■ **FINISHED MEASUREMENTS**
Finished measurements of scarf: 6" wide (not including fringe) X 64" long.

■ **MATERIALS**
BERROCO HIP HOP (100 g) Zion
Scarf—4 hanks
Hat—2 hanks
Mittens—2 hanks
2 St markers
2 St holders

■ **NEEDLES**
Size 13 straight knitting needles
OR SIZE TO OBTAIN GAUGE
Size 5.5 mm crochet hook
Tapestry needle

■ **GAUGE**
10 sts = 4"; 15 rows = 4" in St st on size 13 needles
TAKE TIME TO CHECK GAUGE.

1970 Workbasket

ABBREVIATIONS

beg = begin(ning); **CC** = contrasting color; **ch** = chain; **dc** = double crochet; **dec** = decrease; **inc** = increase; **k** = knit; **lp(s)** = loop(s); **M1**= make one (incr 1); **MC** = main color; **p** = purl; **psso** = pass sl st over k st; **pat(s)** = pattern(s); **rep** = repeat; **RH** = right hand; **RS** = right side; **rnd(s)** = round(s); **sc** = single crochet; **SKP** = sl 1, k 1, psso; **sl** = slip; **st(s)** = stitch(es); **tog** = together; **WS** = wrong side; **yo** = yarn over; **end on WS** = end having just completed a WS row; **end on RS** = end having just completed a RS row.

DIRECTIONS

SCARF

With straight needles, cast on 17 sts.

Row 1 (RS): (K1, p1) twice, k to last 4 sts, end (p1, k1) twice.

Row 2: (P1, k1) twice, p to last 4 sts, end (k1, p1) twice. Rep these 2 rows until piece measures 64" from beg, end on WS. Bind off all sts.

STEAM LIGHTLY: Steam piece lightly by laying piece WS down on a padded surface and move steam iron slowly back and forth 1" above piece. Do not allow iron to touch knitted fabric. Steam will allow knitted fabric to blossom. Selvages and rib-bings will lay flat. This method may not allow you to block pieces larger or smaller.

FINISHING: Cut two 12" long strands of yarn. Put strands tog and fold in half. With crochet hook, draw center of strands through end st on first row of scarf, forming a lp. Pull ends of fringe through this lp. In this manner, make fringe in every other row along 1 entire long edge of scarf. Trim fringe to even off if necessary.

Note: For speedier cutting, wrap yarn multiple times around a piece of cardboard that is the desired finished length of the fringe. Cut the lower edge to free wrapped strands.

With RS facing, using crochet hook, work 1 row dc along opposite long edge of scarf from fringe. Ch 2, turn, work 1 dc in each dc across. Fasten off.

HAT

With straight needles, cast on 26 sts.

Row 1 (RS): (K1, p1) twice, k to last 4 sts, (pl, k1) twice.

Row 2: (p1, k1) twice, p to last 4 sts, (k1, p1) twice. Rep these 2 rows until piece measures 19" from beg, end on WS. Bind off all sts.

FINISHING: Steam piece lightly. Fringe one long edge same as for scarf. Sew cast-on edge to bound-off edge. With tapestry needle, weave yarn through fringed edge of hat 1" in from edge. Draw up tightly to gather, then fasten off.

MITTENS

With straight needles, cast on 22 sts.

Row 1 (RS): K2, * p2, k2, rep from * across.

Row 2: P2, * k2, p2, rep from * across. Rep these 2 rows for 4", end on WS. Work even in St st until piece measures 6" from beg, end on WS.

SHAPE THUMB GUSSET: Next Row (RS): K10, place marker, M1k, k2, M1k, place marker, k to end. Continue to inc 1 st after first marker and before second in this manner every RS row twice more, end on WS—28 sts.

THUMB: Next Row (RS): K to first marker and sl these sts onto first holder, drop marker, k8, drop marker, sl remaining 10 sts onto second holder. Work even in St st on 8 sts until thumb measures 2¼", end on WS.

Dec Row (RS): (K2tog) 4 times—4 sts. Break off yarn, leaving an end for sewing. Draw end through 4 sts on needle and pull up tightly. Fasten off. Sew thumb seam.

HAND: Next Row (RS): Sl 10 sts from first holder onto straight needle, join yarn and pick up and k1 st at base of thumb, k10 sts from second holder—21 sts. Work even in St st until hand measures 5" above thumb, end on WS.

SHAPE TOP: Row 1 (RS): *K2tog, rep from * to last st, k1—11 sts. Purl 1 row.

Row 3: * K2tog, rep from * to last st, k1—6 sts. Purl 1 row. Break off yarn, leaving an end for sewing. Draw end through 6 sts on needle and pull up tightly. Fasten off. Sew mitten seam.

Vintage design.

Sassy Satchel

■ ■ ■

What could be more dramatic than red, except simple black and white in a most striking pattern! Cascade's contemporary fleur-de-lis purse embellished with a Grecian-style geometric border and tassel packs plenty of pizzazz !

■ **PROJECT**
Black & White Fleur-de-lis Purse

■ **SKILL LEVEL**
Intermediate/Advanced

■ **SIZE**
Finished size is 8" across and 5" deep

■ **MATERIALS**
Cascade's Hayfield Yarns (50 g balls)
One ball each White (A) and Black (B)
Next Additions DK Ribbon or any of the Hayfield
DK-weight luxury yarns
One ring marker
One electric hand-mixer (for twisting cord)
One tasseled button
One large snap
Two large paper clips

■ **NEEDLES**
Size 3 (3.25 mm) 16" circular knitting needle

■ **GAUGE**
30 sts = 4"
TAKE TIME TO CHECK GAUGE.

1993 Workbasket

beg = begin(ning); **bet** = between; **BO** = bind off;
CC = contrasting color; **ch** = chain; **CO** = cast on;
dc = double crochet; **dec** = decreas(e)(s)(ing); **eor**
= every other row; **hdc** = half double crochet; **inc** =
increase(e)(s)(ing); **k** = knit; **lp** = loop; **p** = purl;
pat (s) = pattern(s) ; **pm** = place marker; **rnd (s)** =
round (s); **rem** = remaining; **RS** = right side; **sc** =
single crochet; **seq** = sequence; **sk** = skip; **sl st** =
slip stitch; **sp** = space; **SSK** = Sl 2 sts knitwise, insert
point of LH needle through FRONTS of these 2 sts
and k 2 tog; **st(s)** = stitch(es); **St st** = Stockinette
stitch; **wyif** = with yarn in front; **wyib** = with yarn
in back; **WS** = wrong side; **yo** = yarn over; **end on
WS =** end having just completed a WS row; **end on
RS =** end having just completed a RS row.

PATTERN STITCHES

PATTERN 1: In-the-round knitting

Rnd 1: With B, knit.

Rnd 2: With B, purl.

Rnd 3: With A; * sl 1, k5, rep from * around.

Rnd 4 and All Subsequent Even Rows: Purl all
the same sts worked on previous rnd with the same
color; sl all the same sl sts with yarn in *back*.

Rnd 5: With B, k1, sl 1; * k3, sl 1, k1, sl 1; rep from
* around end sl 1.

Rnd 7: With A, sl 1; * k3, sl 1, k1, sl 1; rep from *
around, end sl 1, k1.

Rnd 9: With B, * k3, sl 1, k1, sl 1; rep from *
around.

Rnd 11: With A, k4; * sl 1, k5; rep from * around,
end k1.

Rnd 12: Rep rnd 4.

PATTERN I: Row knitting

Rows 1 and All Odd-Numbered Rows (RS): Work
as for pat 1 in-the-round version.

Rows 2 and All Even-Numbered Rows (WS): Knit
all the same sts worked on previous row with the
same color; sl all the same sl sts with yarn in *front*.

Vintage design.

PATTERN II: In-the-round knitting for main section

SSk: Insert right-hand needle in front of first st on left-hand needle, and in back of next st, k these 2 sts tog.

Note: *Rnds 1, 4, 5, and 8 are in B background and Rows 2, 3, 6, and 7 are the A motif.*

Rnd 1: With B, k2; * (k1, yo, k1) in next st making 3 lps in same st, k3; rep from * around, end last rep k1.

Rnd 2: With A, k2; * sl 3 wyib, k3; rep from * around, end last rep k1.

Rnd 3: With A, k1; * k2 tog, sl 1 wyib, ssk, k1; rep from * around, end last rep ssk.

Rnd 4: With B, * sl 1 wyib, k3; rep from * around.

Rnd 5: With B, * (k1, yo, k1) in next st, k3; rep from * around.

Rnd 6: With A, *sl 3 wyib, k3; rep from * around.

Rnd 7: With A, sl 2 wyib; * ssk, k1, k2 tog, sl 1 wyib; rep from * around. ***Note:*** *2nd st of last k2 tog will be the first sl st.*

Rnd 8: With B, k2; * sl 1 wyib, k3; rep from * around, end last rep with k1.

Rep Rnds 1–8 for Pattern II.

DIRECTIONS

PURSE

With B, CO 120 sts; join, being careful not to twist sts. Place marker at beg of rnd and work Pat I Rnds 1–12, then Rnds 1 and 2 once more.

Next work Pat II until 5" from beg, ending after rnd 8.

Next row, BO first 60 sts, then working back and forth in rows, work in pat I for row knitting for 24 rows for front flap. BO all sts.

TWISTED CORDING FOR STRAP

Cut six 90" lengths of yarn to make one corded strap. Hold tog for each drawstring and knot each end. Fasten a large paperclip through one knot and then into the end of the beater of electric hand mixer. Fasten or have someone hold the other end. Run beater until strand is twisted tightly, gradually moving mixer closer to the other end as tension increases. With tension slightly relaxed (when cord begins to twist on itself), fold in half and allow to wind on itself. Finally, knot each of the double ends.

FINISHING

Sew bottom opening shut. Attach each end of the Twisted Cord strap to each side of bag. Sew tasseled button to center flap. Sew large snap inside flap.

Homespun in Heather

■ ■ ■

As crisp and cozy as an autumn day, this smart heather-soft pullover and tunic ensemble was knit in Lion Brand's Homespun yarn. You won't believe how comfy this casual combo is to wear!

■ **PROJECT**
Heather Pullover & Tunic, by Lion Brand

■ **SKILL LEVEL**
Intermediate

■ **SIZES**
Small (Medium, Large, X-Large, XX-Large)
Directions for Small with larger sizes in parentheses.
If there is only one figure, it applies to all sizes.

■ **FINISHED MEASUREMENT**
Finished chest measurements: 36 (40, 44, 48, 52)"

■ **MATERIALS**
MC—LION BRAND Homespun Sierra (6 oz. skeins)
CC—LION BRAND Homespun Williamsburg Blue
PULLOVER: Homespun 5 (5, 6, 6, 7) skeins
TUNIC: Homespun: 4 (4, 4, 5, 5) skeins;
CC—Homespun 1 (1, 1, 1, 1) skein
3 Large stitch holders
Stitch marker

■ **NEEDLES**
Size 10½ circular needle, 24"
Yarn needle

■ **GAUGE**
3 sts and 4 rows = 1" in St st on 10½ needles
TAKE TIME TO CHECK GAUGE.

1981 Workbasket

ABBREVIATIONS

beg = begin(ning); **CC** = contrasting color; **CO** = cast on; **dec** = decrease; **k** = knit; **M1** = make one (incr 1); **MC** = main color; **p** = purl; **pat** = pattern; **RS** = right side; **ssk** = slip, slip, knit; **sssk** = slip, slip, slip, knit (slip the first, second, and/or third stitch knitwise one at a time, then insert the tip of the left-hand needle into the back of these 2 or 3 sts and knit them together); **st(s)** = stitch(es); **St st** = Stockinette stitch; **tog** = together; **WS** = wrong side.

DIRECTIONS

PULLOVER

Back: ** CO 54 (60, 66, 72, 78) sts. Work 9 rows in k2, p2 rib. Starting with a knit row, work in St st (knit 1 row, purl 1 row) until piece measures 16" from beg or desired length to underarm ending with a purl row.

Armhole Shaping (All Sizes): BO 3 sts at beg of next 2 rows. *For sizes 44, 48, and 52 ONLY:* **Row 1:** ssk, k to last 2 sts, k2tog. **Row 2:** Purl. Repeat Rows 1 and 2 twice more. **

All Sizes: Work even until armhole measures 7 (7½, 8, 8½, 9)".

Neck Shaping: Row 1: k 13 (14, 14, 16, 17), then k 22 (26, 26, 28, 32) and place on large stitch holder, k 13 (14, 14, 16, 17).

Left Shoulder: Row 2: Purl. Row 3: ssk, k to end. **Row 4:** Purl. Bind off.

Right Shoulder: With wrong side facing, join yarn at neck edge. **Row 2:** Purl. **Row 3:** k to last 2 sts, k2tog. **Row 4:** Purl. Bind off.

FRONT

Work same as back from ** to **. Then continue working even until armhole measures 6 (6½, 7, 7½, 8)".

Neck Shaping: Row 1: k 15 (16, 16, 18, 19), then k 18 (22, 22, 24, 28) and place on large stitch holder, k 15 (16, 16, 18, 19).

Right shoulder: **Row 2:** Purl. **Rows 3 and 5:** ssk, k to end. **Rows 4 and 6:** Purl. Bind off.

Left shoulder: Row 2(WS): Join yarn at neck edge, purl across. **Rows 3 and 5:** k to last 2 sts, k2tog. **Rows 4 and 6:** Purl. Bind off.

COLLAR

Sew both shoulder seams. Starting at left shoulder seam, pick up 6 sts along left front neck, k 18 (22, 22, 24, 28) from front stitch holder, pick up 6 sts along right front neck, pick up 4 sts along right back, k 22 (26, 26, 28, 32) from back stitch holder, pick up 4 sts along left back neck: 60 (68, 68, 72, 80) sts. Place marker. Working in rounds, k2, p2 around until collar measures 10". Bind off loosely in rib. Weave in ends.

SLEEVES

CO 28 (28, 28, 32, 32). Work 9 rows in k2, p2 rib.

Row 1 (inc row): K1, M1, k to last st, M1, k1. **Row 2:** Purl. **Row 3:** Knit. **Row 4:** Purl. Rep rows 1–4 3 (4, 5, 6, 6) times more. Then, **Row 1:** K1, M1, k to last st, M1, k1. **Rows 2, 4, and 6:** Purl. **Rows 3 and 5:** Knit. Rep rows 1-6 until you have 48 (52, 54, 58, 60) sts. Work even until sleeve measures 18 (18, 18½, 19, 19)" from beginning. Bind off.

FINISHING

Sew sleeves to armholes between BO sts. *Do not sew upper part of sleeve to the 3 BO sts.* Next, weave or sew BO sts to sides of sleeve. Then, sew side seams and sleeve seams. Weave in ends.

tunic front chart for blue design

10" 11" 12" 13" 14"

Homespun yarn sample colors

TUNIC

BACK

CO 60 (66, 72, 78, 84) sts. Work 9 rows in k2, p2 rib. Starting with knit row, work in St st until piece measures 22" from beg, ending with a purl row.

Armhole Shaping (all sizes): BO 3 sts at beg of next 2 rows.

Next, for sizes 48, 52, and 56 ONLY:
Row 1: Ssk, k to last 2 sts, k2tog. **Row 2:** Purl. Rep rows 1 and 2 twice more.

All Sizes: Work even in St st until armhole measures 8 (8½, 8½, 9, 9)".

Neck Shaping: Row 1: K 13 (15, 15, 16, 19), then k 28 (30, 30, 34, 34) and place on large stitch holder, k 13 (15, 15, 16, 19).

Left shoulder: **Row 2:** Purl. **Row 3:** SSK, k to end. **Row 4:** Purl. Bind off.

Right shoulder: Row 2(WS): Join yarn at neck edge, purl across. **Row 3:** K to last 2 sts, k2tog. **Row 4:** Purl. Bind off.

LEFT FRONT

** CO 30 (32, 36, 38, 42) sts. Work 9 rows in K2, P2 rib. **Row 1:** Inc 1 sts 0 (1, 0, 1, 0) times, k to end: 30 (33, 36, 39, 42) sts. **Row 2:** Purl. Continue in St st until piece measures 6½" from beg ending with a purl row. Join CC and work Chart A over next 9 rows. Then, continue in St st with MC until piece measures 20½" from beg. ** Work Chart A again and AT THE SAME TIME, when 22" from beg and ending with a *purl* row, start Armhole Shaping as follows:

Row 1: BO 3 sts, work across as established. **Row 2:** Purl across as established.

For sizes 48, 52, and 56 ONLY:

Row 3: ssk, knit across as established. **Row 4:** Purl across as established.

Rep rows 3 and 4 twice more. (Remember to keep in pat until you have finished Chart, then continue in MC.)

All Sizes: Work even until armhole measures 7 (7½, 7½, 8, 8)".

Neck Shaping: Row 1: K 13 (15, 15, 16, 19), k2tog, slip remaining 12 (13, 16, 18, 18) sts onto stitch holder. **Rows 2, 4, and 6:** Purl. **Row 3:** K 12 (14, 14, 15, 18), k2tog. **Row 5:** K 11 (13, 13, 14, 17), k2tog. **Row 7:** Knit. **Row 8:** Purl. Bind off.

RIGHT FRONT

Work same as Left Front from ** to **. Then work Chart and AT THE SAME TIME, when 22" from beg and ending with a *knit* row, work as follows:

Armhole Shaping: Row 1: BO 3 sts, purl across as established.

Sizes 40 and 44 ONLY:
Row 2: K across as established.

Sizes 48, 52, and 56 ONLY:
Row 2: Work across as established to last 2 sts, k2tog.

Row 3: Purl across as established.

Rep rows 2 and 3 twice more. (Remember to keep in pat until you have finished Chart, then continue in MC.)

All Sizes: Work even until armhole measures 7 (7½,7½, 8, 8)".

Neck Shaping: Row 1: k 12 (13, 16, 18, 18) sts and place on stitch holder, ssk, k to end: 14 (16, 16, 17, 20) sts on needle. **Rows 2, 4, and 6:** Purl. **Rows 3 and 5:** Ssk, k to end. **Row 7:** Knit. **Row 8:** Purl. Bind off.

NECKBAND

Sew shoulder seams. With right sides facing and beg at right front, k 12 (13, 16, 18, 18) sts from right front stitch holder, pick up 8 sts along right neck to shoulder, pick up 4 sts along right back, k 28 (30, 30, 34, 34) sts from back stitch holder, pick 4 sts along left back to shoulder, pick up 8 sts along left front, k 12 (13, 16, 18, 18) sts from left front stitch holder: 76 (80, 86, 94, 94) sts. Work 3 rows in k2, p2 rib. Bind off loosely in rib.

FRONT BANDS

From right side of work, pick up 92 sts evenly spaced along left front and then right front. Work 3 rows in k2, p2 rib. Bind off in rib.

ARMBANDS

Working between the 3 BO sts, pick up 68 (68, 68, 72, 72) sts. Work 3 rows in k2, p2 rib. Bind off in rib. Sew sides of band to the Bind off sts.

FINISHING

Sew side seams up to armbands. Weave in ends.

Poignant Picots

■ ■ ■

Wedding garters have a long tradition and so does tatting. Try this quick-and-easy but elegant tatted wedding garter with a delicate picot pattern. Designed by Handy Hands based on a Workbasket *1978 design.*

■ **PROJECT**
Tatted Bridal Garter, by Handy Hands

■ **SKILL LEVEL**
Beginner

■ **SIZE**
Tat length to fit

■ **MATERIALS**
Flora size 10 thread, color of your choice
Needle Ribbon, at least a yard (enough to thread through tatted length and tie in graceful bow)
Tatting shuttle or needle

ABBREVIATIONS

R = Ring(s); **Rw** = Row; **Ch** = Chain(s); **Cl** = Close ring.

DIRECTIONS:

Note: *See How-To-Tat Basics beginning on page 120 for more information and diagrams.*

R 8-8 Cl. Rw.

Ch 5-1-1-1-1-1-5 Rw.

R 4-4+ (to center picot of prev. R) 4-4 Cl. Rw.

*Ch 4-1-1-4 Cl.

R 4+ (to last picot of prev. R) 4-4-4 Cl. Rw.*

Repeat for * to * for desired length.

1978 Workbasket

Ch 5-1-1-1-1-1-5 Rw.

R 8+ (to center picot of prev. R) 8 Cl. Rw.

Ch 5-1-1-1-1-1-5 Rw.

R 4-4+ (to center joining picot of prev. R) 4-4 Cl. Rw.

**Ch 4-1-1-4 Cl.

R 4+ (to last picot of prev. R) 4+ (to center picot of corresponding R) 4-4 Cl. Rw. **

Repeat for ** to ** to end.

Ch 5-1-1-1-1-1-5 Rw.

Join to the beginning. Tie/Hide/Cut

Thread ribbon (type and color of your choice) through middle of tatted length. Tie both ends in graceful bow. If desired, can also embellish with tiny silk roses (as shown).

Linear á la Mode

Believe it or not, a beginner can make this gorgeous sweater! Echoing a sweater in a 1977 Workbasket *issue, the new Tahki Stacy Charles version is in cashmere-soft Micio in seven glorious colors. Earn* **these** *stripes the easy way!*

■ **PROJECT**
Striped Fuzzy Sweater, by Tahki Stacy Charles

■ **SKILL LEVEL**
Beginner

■ **SIZES**
Small (Medium, Large)
Directions for Small with larger sizes in parentheses.
If there is only one figure, it applies to all sizes.

■ **FINISHED MEASUREMENTS**
Finished Chest: 33 (35, 37)"
Length: 20 (20½, 21)"
Upper Arm: 13 (13, 13½)"

■ **MATERIALS**
TAHKI STACY CHARLES Collezione Micio yarn (each ball 50 g; approx. 110 yds)
A—3 balls black for all sizes
B—1 ball red for all sizes
C—1 ball rust for all sizes
D—1 ball brown for all sizes
E—1 ball purple for all sizes
F—1 ball olive for all sizes
G—1 ball sage green for all sizes
Stitch holders

■ **NEEDLES**
Size 8 knitting needles
OR SIZE TO OBTAIN GAUGE
Size 6 needles for neck finishing

1977 Workbasket

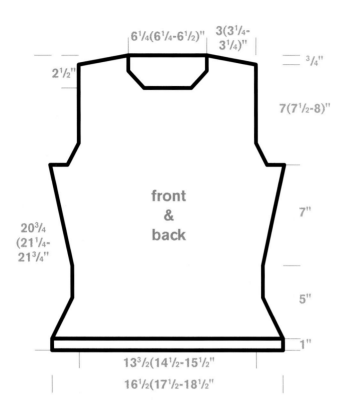

6¼(6¼-6½)" 3(3¼-3¼)"

2½"

20¾(21¼-21¾)"

front & back

¾"

7(7½-8)"

7"

5"

1"

13½(14½-15½)"

16½(17½-18½)"

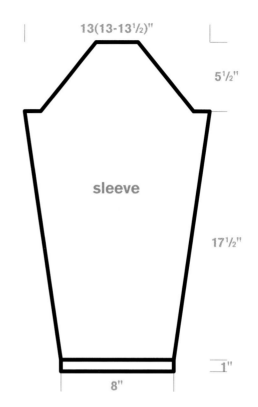

13(13-13½)"

sleeve

5½"

17½"

1"

8"

GAUGE

16 sts and 24 rows = 4" in St st using size 8 needles
TAKE TIME TO CHECK GAUGE.

ABBREVIATIONS

beg = begin(ning); **bet** = between; **BO** = bind off; **CC** = contrasting color; **ch** = chain; **CO** = Cast on; **cont** = continue; **dc** = double crochet; **dec** = decreas(e)(s)(ing); **eor** = every other row; **inc** = increase(e)(s)(ing); **k** = knit; **lp** = loop; **MC** = main color; **p** = purl; **pat** = pattern; **pm** = place marker; **rem** = remaining; **RS** = right side; **sc** = single crochet; **seq** = sequence; **sk** = skip; **ssk** = slip, slip, knit; **sssk** = slip, slip, slip, knit (slip the first, second, and/or third stitch knitwise one at the time, then insert the tip of the left-hand needle into the back of these 2 or 3 sts and knit them together); **st(s)** = stitch(es); **St st** = Stockinette stitch; **tog** = together; **wyif** = with yarn in front; **wyib** = with yarn in back; **WS** = wrong side; **yo** = yarn over.

DIRECTIONS

STRIPE SEQUENCE

Working in St st (k 1 row, p 1 row), work *2 rows A, 4 rows B, 2 rows A, 4 rows C, 2 rows A, 4 rows D, 2 rows A, 4 rows E, 2 rows A, 4 rows F, 2 rows A, 4 rows G; rep from * for length.

BACK

Using larger needles and A, cast on 74 (78, 82) sts; work 1" in k2, p2 rib, end WS row. Cont with A, beg Stripe pat, work 2 rows even.

Shape Body: Dec 1 st each side every 4 rows 6 times—62 (66, 70) sts. Work even until piece measures 6" from beg, then inc 1 st each side every 4 rows 6 times—74 (78, 82) sts. Work even in Stripe pat until piece measures 13" from beg, end with 4th row of G.

Shape armhole: Cont in Stripe pat, at each side, bind off 4 sts once, 3 sts once, then 1 st each side every other row 3 (3, 4) times—54 (58, 60) sts. Work even in Stripe pat until armhole measures 7 (7½, 8)", end WS row.

Shape Shoulder: At each shoulder, bind off 6 (7, 7) sts once, 7 (8, 8) sts once; place rem sts on holder for black neck.

FRONT

Work as for back until armhole measures 4½ (5, 5½)", end WS row.

Shape Neck: (RS) Cont in Stripe pat, k18 (20, 20) sts, place next 18 (18, 20) sts on a holder, join a second ball of yarn and work to end. Working each side separately, bind off at each neck edge 3 sts once, then 1 st at each neck edge every other row twice—13 (15, 15) sts each shoulder; when piece measures same as back to shoulder shaping, Shape shoulders as for Back.

SLEEVES

Using larger needles and A, cast on 36 sts; work 4 rows in k2, p2 rib. Beg Stripe pat with 4 rows B.

Shape Sleeve: Cont in Stripe pat, inc 1 st each side every 6 rows 4 (4, 5) times, every 8 rows 7 times— 58 (58, 60) sts. Work even until piece measures approx 18½" from beg, end with 4th row of G.

Shape Cap: At each side, bind off 4 sts once; then 1 st each side every other row until cap measures 5" from beg of shaping; at each side, bind off 2 sts twice; bind off rem sts.

FINISHING

Block pieces very lightly to finished measurements. Sew right shoulder seam.

Mock Turtleneck: RS facing, using smaller needles and A, beg at left front neck edge, pick up and knit approx 68 (68, 72) sts evenly around neck, including sts on holders; work in k2, p2 rib for 3"; bind off in pat.

Sew left shoulder and mock turtleneck. Set in sleeves; sew side and sleeve seams.

Vintage design.

Ripple Effect

Ripples were the rage in '70s fashions and they're back in waves! This dramatic redeux by Lion Brand sports a mesmerizing ripple stitch in rich Wool Ease colors. Sure to make a splash in any circle!

■ **PROJECT**
Ripple Pullover, by Lion Brand

■ **SKILL LEVEL**
Intermediate

■ **SIZES**
Small (Medium, Large, X-Large, XX-Large)
Directions for Small with larger sizes in parentheses.
If there is only one figure, it applies to all sizes.

■ **FINISHED MEASUREMENTS**
Finished chest: 39 (42, 45, 48, 51)"
Length: 24 (24, 25, 25, 26)"

■ **MATERIALS**
Lion Brand Wool-Ease (3 oz. balls, approx. 197 yd)
A/MC—Cranberry 4 (4, 5, 5, 5) balls
B—Butterscotch 2 (2, 3, 3, 3) balls
C—Black 2 (2, 3, 3, 3) balls
D—Seaspray 2 (2, 3, 3, 3) balls
E—Fisherman 2 (2, 3, 3, 3) balls
F—Loden 2 (2, 3, 3, 3) balls

■ **NEEDLES**
Size I-9 (5.5 mm) crochet hook or
SIZE TO OBTAIN GAUGE
Size G-6 (4 mm) crochet hook for joining seams
Large-eyed, blunt needle

■ **GAUGE**
8 "V" sts + 10 rows = 4".
For gauge swatch Ch 34, work "V" st pattern.
TAKE TIME TO CHECK GAUGE.

1975 Workbasket

DIRECTIONS

"V" STITCH PATTERN (Multiple of 3 +1, plus 3 ch to turn)

Row 1: 2 dc in 5th ch from hook—"V" st made. (Skip 2 ch, 2 dc in next ch) across to last 2 ch. Skip 1 ch, dc in last ch, ch 3, turn.

Row 2: (Skip 2 sts, 2 dc in middle of "V" st below) across, ending with 1 dc in t-ch space. Ch 3, turn.

Repeat Row 2 for pattern.

NOTES

1. 2 dc worked in one space counts as one "V" st.

2. Last dc at end of each row and t-ch at beg of row count as edge sts.

3. When changing colors at end of row, work last dc until 2 loops remain on hook. Tie new color around old color and slide knot close to hook. Draw new color through 2 loops on hook to complete st. Leave 6" yarn ends at edges to be worked with when finishing sweater.

4. To inc 1 "V" st work 2 dc in space formed by edge st.

5. When working sc along row ends, a pattern of (2 sc in space, 1 sc in next space) may be needed to ease in fullness.

6. To dec 1 sc draw up loop in each of next 2 sc, yo, draw through 3 loops on hook.

COLOR SEQUENCE

3 rows	A Cranberry
1 row	B Butterscotch
1 row	C Black
2 rows	D Seaspray
1 row	A Cranberry
1 row	E Fisherman
1 row	F Loden
1 row	A Cranberry
2 rows	B Butterscotch
1 row	D Seaspray
1 row	C Black
1 row	E Fisherman
1 row	F Loden

LION BRAND'S Wool-Ease yarn comes in a vast variety of colors and weights. Shown is just a smattering of Wool-Ease colors and weights.

BACK

With A and larger hook, ch 118 (127, 136, 145, 154). Work in pattern, forming 38 (41, 44, 47, 50) "V" sts across, plus an edge st at each end, changing colors in sequence as indicated, until piece measures 14" (or desired length) to underarm. At end of last row, ch 1, turn.

Shape Armhole: Slip st across first 9 dc, ch 3, continue in "V" st pattern across 30 (33, 36, 39, 42) "V" sts, skip 1 dc, dc in next dc for edge st, ch 3, turn (leaving last 3 full "V" sts unworked). Continue in pattern until piece measures 9 (9½, 10, 10½, 11)" from beg of armhole. Fasten off.

FRONT

Work same as for Back and armhole shaping. Continue in pattern until piece measures 6 (6½, 7, 7½, 8)" from beg of armhole.

Shape Neck: (Note: When changing colors for the following rows, leave long enough yarn ends at neck edge to weave in across entire row toward armhole edge.)

Next Row: Work in pattern across 9 (9, 10, 11, 12) "V" sts, skip 1 dc, dc in next dc for edge st, ch 3, turn. Continue in pattern until piece measures 9 (9½, 10, 10½, 11)" from beg of armhole. Change to A, ch 1, turn, sc in each dc across and in t-ch—20 (20, 22, 24, 26) sc. Fasten off, leaving long yarn end for sewing shoulder seam. Attach yarn to last row worked before neck shaping (WS facing) with slip st in the 42nd (48th, 52nd, 56th, 60th) dc from beg of row, counting t-ch at beg as 1 dc. Ch 3, continue in pattern as for other side, leaving center 10 (13, 14, 15, 16) "V" sts unworked. Fasten off, leaving long yarn end for sewing shoulder seam.

SLEEVES

With A and larger hook, ch 55 (55, 61, 61, 61). Work even in pattern, forming 17 (17, 19, 19, 19) "V" sts across plus an edge st at each end, changing

Vintage design.

colors in sequence as indicated, for 4 (4, 4, 3, 3) rows. Inc 1 "V" st at each end of next row and every 5th (5th, 5th, 4th, 4th) row thereafter until there are 35 (37, 39, 41, 43) "V" sts across. Work even for 5 (0, 0, 6, 2) more rows for a total of 50 rows from beg (approximately 20"). Change to color A yarn, ch 1, turn, sc in each dc across and in t-ch—72 (76, 80, 84, 88) sc. Fasten off, leaving long yarn end for sewing sleeve to body.

FINISHING

Sew shoulder seams.

Neckband: Rnd 1: Join A with slip st at center back neck, ch 1, work sc evenly around neck edge. Join rnd with slip st in first sc, ch 1, turn. **Rnd 2:** Sc in each sc around, decreasing 1 sc at inner curves. Join rnd, ch 1, turn. **Rnd 3:** Hdc in each sc around, join rnd, fasten off.

Armhole and Sleeve Seams: With A, work 1 row sc evenly along armhole edge of body of sweater to correspond with the number of sts along last sleeve row. Set in sleeve and sew to armhole edge.

Sleeve and Seams: With A and smaller hook, and right sides together, attach yarn at cuff edge with slip st through both layers. Working tightly, (ch 3, slip st in next space through both layers) along sleeve seam to underarm and down side seam to lower edge. Hold yarn ends toward back, being careful not to catch them in slip sts.

Lower Edge and Cuff Borders: Join A with slip st at seam, ch 1, work (1 hdc in center of "V" st, 1 hdc in next space) around edge, join rnd with slip st, fasten off.

Yarn Ends: On inside of sweater, tie pairs of corresponding color yarn ends (one each from front and back) together with overhand knots. Yarn ends within 3" to 4" of lower edge and cuffs may be sewn into seams, all others may be trimmed to about 3".

Checkmate!

■ ■ ■

Workbasket's 1967 checked sweater is fun, but Coats & Clark's contemporary tweed pattern, rendered in Red Heart yarn, has stunning checkerboard charm. Definitely a smart move in the game of style!

■ PROJECT
Checkerboard Sweater, by Coats & Clark

■ SKILL LEVEL
Intermediate

■ SIZE
Small (Medium, Large)
Directions for Small with larger sizes in parentheses.
If there is only one figure, it applies to all sizes.

■ FINISHED MEASUREMENTS
To Fit Chest: 32 (36, 40)"
Finished Chest Measurement: 36 (40, 44)"

■ MATERIALS
COATS & CLARK Red Heart Yarn
A—5 (5, 6) skeins, Red Heart Tweed Worsted-Weight
Yarn (4 oz. skeins) Lavender
B—2 (2, 3) skeins, Red Heart Super-Saver Worsted-
Weight (8 oz. skeins) Soft White

■ NEEDLES
Susan Bates crochet hooks
Size G-6 (4 mm)
Size H-8 (5 mm)
OR SIZE TO OBTAIN GAUGE.

■ GAUGE
13 sts = 4", 33 rows = 7" with larger hook.
TAKE TIME TO CHECK GAUGE.

1967 Workbasket

ABBREVIATIONS

beg = begin(ning); **cont** = continue; **est** = established; **pat** = pattern; **rem** = remaining; **rep** = repeat; **st(s)** = stitch(es); **ch** = chain; **sc** = single crochet; **hdc** = half double crochet; **dc** = double crochet; **fpdc** = front post double crochet; **bpdc** = back post double crochet; **lp** = loop; **sk** = skip; **sp** = space; **dec** = decrease; **RS** = right side; **WS** = wrong side; ***** = repeat whatever follows the * as indicated; **[ ]** = work directions given in brackets the number of times specified.

DIRECTIONS

CHART INSTRUCTIONS

RS rows are worked from right to left. WS rows are worked from left to right. * Work 1 row using A drop loop from hook. Go back to beginning of last row and work 1 row using B working in the same direction. Drop loop from hook. Pick up dropped loop of A. Repeat from * throughout. Begin each row with ch 2 (does not count as a st) and sc in first st even if chart does not have a sc indicated for the first st. End each row with a sc in the last st even if chart does not have a sc indicated for the last st. When working long single crochet = ls, work ls in sc or ls st in row or rows below working over ch st. Never work ls in ch st except in beginning foundation ch.

BACK

With larger hook using A ch 60 (66, 72). Begin by working first sc in second ch from hook.

Follow chart for Back until piece is 22½ (23½, 24½)" ending with a WS A row.

Shape Shoulders: Work next pat row for 20 (22, 24) st. Fasten off. Skip next 19 (21, 23) st. Attach yarn in next st, ch 1, continue across row in est pat. Fasten off. Using A, sc in each st across both shoulders. Fasten off.

FRONT

Work same as Back until 14 rows less than back ending on a WS A row.

First Shoulder Shaping: Work next pat row for 24 (26, 28) st; turn.

Cont working in est pat until 1 row less than Back, at the same time, dec 2 st at next edge on next B row then 1 st at neck edge on next 2 B rows.

Using A, sc in each st across shoulder. Fasten off.

Second Shoulder Shaping: Sk next 11 (13, 15) st. Rep as for First Shoulder.

stitch chart schematic for lavender checkerboard sweater

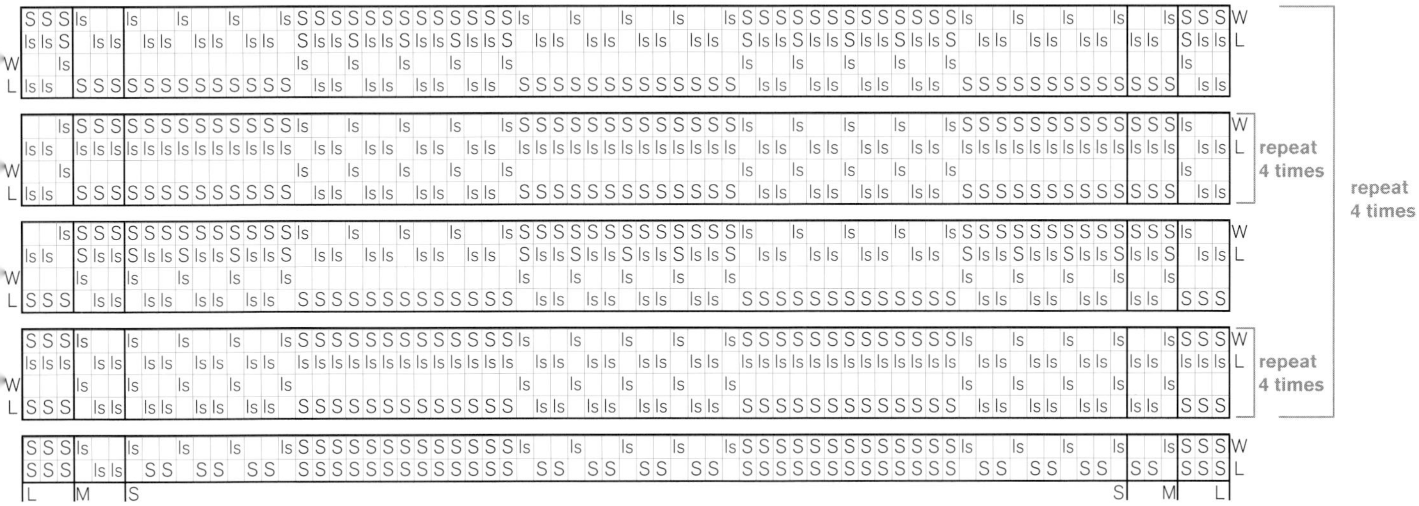

[stitch chart grid — complex checkerboard pattern of S, ls, S, W, L symbols arranged in rows; "repeat 4 times" noted at right for two sections, with a larger "repeat 4 times" bracket to the far right; row markers W, L on the left and right sides; bottom markers L, M, S and S, M, L]

Legend:

S	SINGLE CROCHET	L	SINGLE CROCHET
ls	LONG SINGLE CROCHET	W	LONG SINGLE CROCHET
	CHAIN STITCH		

SLEEVES

Put mark 9 (10, 11)" down from shoulder on front and back. With RS facing, using larger hook, attach A at mark. Ch 1, work first row of chart evenly spaced between markers. Cont working chart till 4 (3, 2)" from beg.

Cont working chart, at the same time dec 1 st on end of every B row till 15 (15½, 16)" from beg ending with a B row.

Using A, sc in each st across. Fasten off.

Sew side and sleeve seams.

SLEEVE and BOTTOM RIBBING

Rnd 1: With RS facing, attach A at opening, with smaller hook ch 2 (counts as 1 hdc), work an even number of hdc evenly spaced around opening, join in top of beg ch 2. **Rnd 2:** Ch 2, * fpdc around post of next st, bpdc around post of next st, rep from * to last st, fpdc around post of last st, join in top of beg ch 2.

Rep Rnd 2 till ribbing is 2". Fasten off.

NECK RIBBING

With RS facing, attach A at neck, with smaller hook ch 2 (counts as 1 hdc), work an even number of hdc evenly spaced around neck opening, join in top of beg ch 2. Rep Rnd 2 of Sleeve and Bottom Ribbing for 1". Fasten off.

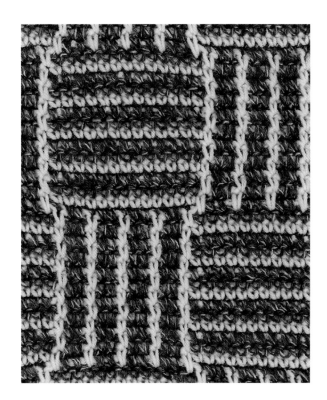

Sweater-Coat Swank

■ ■ ■

This gorgeously textured sweater with cozy cowl neck by Cascade is done in Magnum wool yarn. Quite similar in design to a **Workbasket** *December 1970 popcorn coat, the svelte sweater-coat look was classic then and still is!*

■ PROJECT
Sweater Coat, by Cascade

■ SKILL LEVEL
Intermediate

■ SIZE
Small (Medium, Large)
Directions for Small with larger sizes in parentheses.
If there is only one figure, it applies to all sizes.

■ FINISHED MEASUREMENTS
Finished Chest: 48 (54, 60)"
Length hanging: 48" (Coat can stretch, so plan ahead regarding length.)

■ MATERIALS
CASCADE's Magnum yarn 10 (11, 12) skeins
CASCADE 220 yarn 8 (9, 10) skeins
5 large buttons and 3 medium matching buttons

■ NEEDLES
Sizes 8, 9, 10, 10½ & 15 (The size 9 must be a long circular needle.)

■ GAUGE
In pattern stitch, 7 sts = 13½"
TAKE TIME TO CHECK GAUGE.

1970 **Workbasket**

ABBREVIATIONS

beg = begin(ning); **bet** = between; **BO** = bind off; **CC** = contrasting color; **ch** = chain; **CO** = Cast on; **dc** = double crochet; **dec** = decreas(e)(s)(ing); **eor** = every other row; **inc** = increase (s)(ing); **k** = knit; **lp** = loop; **MC** = main color; **p** = purl; **pat** = pattern; **pm** = place marker; **rem** = remaining; **RS** = right side; **sc** = single crochet; **seq** = sequence; **sk** = skip; **ssk** = slip, slip, knit; **sssk** = slip, slip, slip, knit (slip the first, second, and/or third stitch knitwise, one at the time, then insert the tip of left-hand needle into the back of these 2 or 3 sts and knit them together); **st(s)** = stitch (es); **St st** = Stockinette stitch; **wyif** = with yarn in front; **wyib** = with yarn in back; **WS** = wrong side; **yo** = yarn over.

DIRECTIONS

PATTERN STITCH

When working with Magnum and 220, always use one strand of each for pattern stitch. The 220 is always used two strands for trim ribbing. For a softer lighter coat, use Magnum alone for pattern stitch, and you will use three skeins less of Cascade 220.

Pattern Stitch for Magnum and 220:
Row 1: (k2, p2) rep. to end
Row 2: Purl
Row 3: (p2, k2) rep. to end
Row 4: Purl

Trim Ribbing:
Row 1: (k2, p2) rep. to end
Row 2: Knit the knits & Purl the purls

Note: Always keep in the Magnum pattern stitch, a selvedge stitch of one knit at the beginning and end of right side rows. Make all increases and decreases inside that edge stitch.

Vintage design.

BACK

Cast on very loosely 56 (60, 68) sts and with size 15 needles work pattern stitch. Work pattern decreasing 1 st each end every 6", 4 times 48 (52, 60) sts. When total from beginning is 38", or desired length, shape armholes.

Bind off 3 sts at the beginning of the next 2 rows. Then bind off 1 (2, 3) sts beginning next 2 rows 40 (42, 48) sts. Then decrease 1 st each end every other row 1 (1, 3) times. Work even on 38 (40, 42) sts until armhole measures 9" from the first bind off.

Shape Shoulder: Bind off 4 sts at the beginning of the next 6 rows, then bind off remaining 14 (16, 18) sts.

LEFT FRONT

Cast on very loosely 26 (28, 32) sts, and work pattern stitch on size 15 needles. Dec 1 st at the armhole edge every 8" 3 times. When the front is the same as the back to the armhole (count your rows, it's easy in this pattern), bind off 1 (2, 3) sts at armhole edge, then decrease 1 (2, 3) sts at armhole edge every other row. When armhole measures 5½", shape neck. Bind off 4 (5, 6) sts, then decrease 1 st on next row. Skip 1 row, decrease 1 st at neck edge. When front measures the same as back, shape shoulders. Bind off 4 sts on armhole edge only 6 times, then bind off remaining sts.

Photo: Courtesy of Cascade Yarns.

POCKETS

Cast on very loosely 10 (12, 12) sts with size 15 needles and work pattern st. At 5 (5½, 5½)" on wrong side row, change to 220 and size 9 needle. Increase 1 st in every stitch. 20 (24, 24) sts. Work in 2/2 rib for 4 rows, bind off loosely. For 2nd pocket, begin pattern st in reverse for 1st size only, and reverse rib pattern for 2nd and 3rd sizes.

FINISHING

Lightly steam all pieces. **Left front border:** with 220 and size 9 needles and right side facing, pick up 128 sts just inside the selvedge edge. For different lengths, pick up 1 st in every row hole, making sure you have an even number. Work 2/2 rib pattern for 9 rows and bind off in pattern loosely. **Right front border:** After placing buttons on left front, work right border same as for left placing buttonholes where needed. (A yarn over buttonhole works well.) Join the front and back shoulder seams.

COLLAR

Note: *Do not pick up sts in the top edges of front borders. A perpendicular border will be put on the collar, which will be joined later.*

With size 8 needles and 220, beginning at Magnum pattern neck edge, with right side facing, pick up 74 (74, 78) sts as follows: 26 (26, 27) along front neck edge, 22 (22, 24) across back of neck, and 26 (26, 27) along front neck edge.

Work in 2/2 rib pattern for 3". Change to size 9 needles and work for another 3". Change to size 10 needles and work for 3" more. Change to size 10½ needles and at 10 (11, 11)" bind off very loosely in rib pattern.

Collar Borders: Left: At front edge of collar with size 9 needles and 220, pick up 38 (42, 42) sts.

(***Note:*** *It may be smoother to pick up in every row and reduce evenly on the first rib row.*) Work 9 rows in 2/2 rib pattern. Bind off loosely in rib pat. Repeat for right edge, placing buttonholes where needed.

Place medium button ½" from outside edge and 2 more 2½" apart.

Sew collar borders to respective front borders. Weave side and sleeve seams. Sew sleeves into armholes.

RIGHT FRONT

Work as for left front, remembering to reverse all shaping.

SLEEVES

Cast on very loosely 22 (24, 26) sts and work pattern st on size 15 needles. Increase 1 st each edge every 2" 6 times. 34 (36, 38) sts. When sleeve measures 16" or desired length to underarm shape, cap as follows:

Bind off 2 (3, 3) sts at beginning of the next 2 rows. Then decrease 1 st each end every other row 6 (6, 7) times (14 sts). Work even for 6 rows. Bind off 2 sts at the beginning of the next 4 rows, then bind off remaining sts.

Retro's the Rage!

■ ■ ■

Retro is **de riguer** *in fashion today and classic crochet '60s vests are back in spades! Lion Brand's flashy and fashionable jiffy vest, done in luscious lime Microspun, is short on time and effort to make, but long on style!*

■ PROJECT:
60s Jiffy Crochet Vest, by Lion Brand

■ SKILL LEVEL
Beginner

■ SIZE
One size fits most.
Finished chest: 48"
Tied length: 27"

■ MATERIALS
LION BRAND Microspun (2½ oz 168 yd balls)
5 balls Lime or color of your choice

■ NEEDLES
Size J-10 (6 mm) crochet hook
OR SIZE TO OBTAIN GAUGE

■ GAUGE
17 sts + 8 rows = 4"
TAKE TIME TO CHECK GAUGE.

1967 Workbasket

ABBREVIATIONS

beg = begin(ning); **ch** = chain; **cont** = continu(e)(ing); **dc** = double crochet; **dec** = decreas(e)(s)(ing); **foll** = follow(s)(ing); **rnd(s)** = round(s); **RS** = right side; **sc** = single crochet; **st(s)** = stitch(es); **t-ch** = turning chain; **WS** = wrong side.

DIRECTIONS

NOTE: Body is worked in one piece.

PATTERN STITCH

Row 1: 1 dc in 6th ch from hook (counts as 2 sts), *ch 1, skip 1 ch, 1 dc in next ch; rep from * across.

Row 2: Ch 3, turn. *1 dc in ch-1 space, ch 1, skip 1 dc; rep from * across, end 1 dc in ch-1 space, ch 1, 1 dc in 2nd ch of beg ch of previous row.

Row 3: Ch 3, turn. *1 dc in ch-1 space, ch 1, skip 1 dc; rep from * across, end 1 dc in top of t-ch.

Row 4: Ch 3, turn. *1 dc in ch-1 space, ch 1, skip 1 dc; rep from * across, end 1 dc in last ch-space, ch 1, 1 dc in 3rd ch of t-ch.

Rep Rows 3 and 4 for pattern.

BODY

Ch 208. Beg with pattern Row 1 (204) sts, work even until piece measures 15" from beg.

Next Row: Place markers 51 sts from each side for side seams. Cont until piece measures 16" from beg.

Shape V-Neck: Keeping to pattern, dec 1 st at beg and end of each row (center front) 17 times. AT SAME TIME, when piece measures 17" from beg, beg shaping armhole.

Right Front (RS): Work to within 13 sts of right side-seam marker (armhole edge), turn. Dec 1 st at armhole edge every other row 4 times and cont neck decs. Work until armhole measures 10" from beg. Fasten off.

BACK

With RS facing, join yarn 13 sts in from right side-seam marker, ch 3, then keeping to pattern work across to within 13 sts of left side-seam marker, turn. Dec 1 st at beg and end of every other row 4 times for armholes. Work even until armholes measure 10" from beg. Fasten off.

LEFT FRONT

With RS facing, join yarn 13 sts in from left side-seam marker (armhole edge), ch 3 and cont in pat-

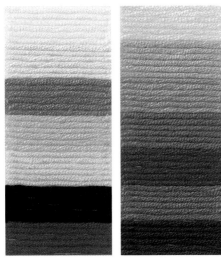

Lion Brand's vest is crocheted in
MicroSpun yarn available in a wide range
of brilliant colors.

Vintage design: Long Crochet vests were the rage in the '60s and '70s. Shown are just a few of the many
Workbasket vest featured.

tern, dec 1 st at armhole edge every other row 4
times and cont neck decs. Work until armhole
measures 10" from beg. Fasten off.

FINISHING

Sew fronts to back at shoulders over 17 sts. Work 1
row sc around entire outer edge of Vest, working 3
sc in front corners.

ARMHOLE EDGING

Join yarn at underarm marker and work 1 rnd sc
around armhole. Fasten off.

TIES

Make two. Ch 57. **Row 1:** Sc in 2nd ch from hook
and in each ch across (56 sc). Fasten off, leaving a
long strand to join to Vest at V-neck shaping.

The 'Scoop' on Style

■ ■ ■

*Scoopnecks are sensuous and breezy in **any** color, but Tahki Stacy Charles' dramatic pullover in its variegated Austermann Domani yarn is a veritable whirlwind of splashy tropical hues!*

■ PROJECT
Scoopneck Sweater, by Tahki Stacy Charles

■ SKILL LEVEL
Intermediate

■ SIZE:
Small (Medium)
Directions for Small with Medium size in parentheses.
If there is only one figure, it applies to both sizes.

■ MATERIALS
TAHKI STACY CHARLES Austermann Domani Kolibri
5 (6) balls (each ball 50 g)
Stitch holders

■ NEEDLES
Size 7 (4.5mm) knitting needles
Size 6 (4 mm) crochet hook

■ GAUGE
14 sts and 23 rows = 4" over St st.
TAKE TIME TO CHECK GAUGE.

1985 Workbasket

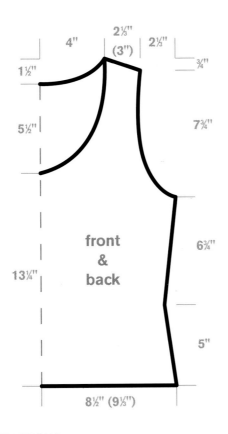

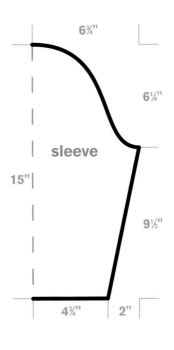

ABBREVIATIONS

beg = begin(ning); **bet** = between; **BO** = bind off; **CC** = contrasting color; **ch** = chain; **CO** = Cast on; **dc** = double crochet; **dec** = decreas(e)(s)(ing); **eor** = every other row; **inc** = increase(e)(s)(ing); **k** = knit; **lp** = loop; **MC** = main color; **p** = purl; **pat** = pattern; **pm** = place marker; **rem** = remaining; **RS** = right side; **sc** = single crochet; **seq** = sequence; **sk** = skip; **ssk** = slip, slip, knit; **sssk** = slip, slip, slip, knit (slip the first, second, and/or third stitch knitwise one at the time, then insert the tip of left-hand needle into the back of these 2 or 3 sts and knit them together); **st(s)** = stitch(es); **St st** = Stockinette stitch; **tog** = together; **wyif** = with yarn in front; **wyib** = with yarn in back; **WS** = wrong side; **yo** = yarn over.

DIRECTIONS

BACK

Cast on 64 (70) sts and work in garter st for 4 rows.

Row 5: 1 selvage st, *K2tog, yo, rep from *, end with 1 selvage st.

Row 6: Purl. Cont in St st, dec 1 st each side every 8th row 3 times = 58 (64) sts. Inc 1 st each side every 13th row 3 times = 64 (70) sts. Work even until piece measures 12" from beg.

Shape Armholes: Bind off 3 sts at beg of next 2 rows, 2 sts at beg of next 2 rows, dec 1 st each side every 2nd row 3 times = 48 (54) sts. Work even until piece measures 19" from beg.

Shape Neck and Shoulder: Bind off center 10 sts and working both sides at once, bind off from each neck edge 4 sts once, 2 sts once and 1 st once. AT THE SAME TIME, when piece measures 19½" from beg, bind off from each shoulder edge 4 (5) sts 3 times.

FRONT

Work same as back until piece measures 13¼" from beg.

Shape Neck: Bind off center 8 sts and, working both sides at once, bind off from each neck edge 3 sts once, 2 sts once and 1 st 3 times. When same length as back to shoulder, shape shoulder same as back.

SLEEVES

Cast on 36 sts and work first 6 rows same as back. Work in St st, inc 1 st each side every 7th row 7 times = 50 sts. Work even until piece measures 9½" from beg.

Shape Cap: Bind off 3 sts at beg of next 4 rows, 1 st at beg of next 2 rows, dec 1 st each side every 4th row 4 times, every 2nd row 4 times and bind off 2 sts at beg of next 4 rows. Bind off rem sts.

Vintage design.

FINISHING

Block pieces to finished measurements. Sew shoulder seams. Set in sleeves. Sew side and sleeve seams. With RS facing and crochet hook, work 1 rnd sc evenly around neck edge.

Cabled Cache

■ ■ ■

This alluring cabled shell with sweeping yoke by Cascade Yarns echoes **Workbasket**'s *1968 design. But the contemporary version is brilliantly updated in bold chartreuse Indulgency yarn. A cable classic in any decade!*

■ **PROJECT**
Cabled Shell with Yoke, by Cascade

■ **SKILL LEVEL**
Advanced

■ **SIZE**
Medium (Large)
Directions for Medium with Large size in parentheses.
If there is only one figure, it applies to both sizes.

■ **FINISHED MEASUREMENTS**
Medium to fit 32" to 36" bust
Large to fit 38" to 42" bust

■ **MATERIALS**
Cascade Indulgency Yarn 3 (4) skeins
Color of your choice

■ **NEEDLES**
Size 7 circular needles, 16" and 24"
Size 4 circular needs, 16" and 24"

■ **GAUGE**
7 sts = #1" over cable pattern on size 7 needles.
TAKE TIME TO CHECK GAUGE.

1968 Workbasket

beg = begin(ning); **dec** = decrease; **k** = knit; **p** = purl; **RS** = right side; **st(s)** = stitch(es); **ssk** = slip, slip, knit; **sssk** = slip, slip, slip, knit (slip the first, second, and/or third stitch knitwise one at the time, then insert the tip of left-hand needle into the back of these 2 or 3 sts and knit them together); **WS** = wrong side.

DIRECTIONS

NOTES

Do not stretch to measure your test swatch.

The body is worked in the round up to the arm-holes.

Ribbings (armbands, bottom) are worked in garter st in the round.

Collar is also garter st in the round.

BODY

With 24" size 4 needles, cast on 205 (240) sts. Work in the round as follows: (knit 1 round, purl 1 round) repeat 2 more times. On the last round, knit and increase to 240 (280) sts evenly spaced. Change to 24" size 7 needles and start working in pattern as follows:

CABLE PATTERN

c8b = slip next 4 sts on cable needle and hold in the back of your work. K 4 sts, then k the 4 sts on the cable needle.

Row 1: p1, (k8, p2) rep around ending with p1.

Row 2: p1, (c8b, p2, k8, p2) rep. around ending with p1.

Row 3: as row 1.

Row 4: as row 1.

Row 5: as row 1.

Row 6: as row 2.

Row 7: as row 1

Row 8: as row 1.

Row 9: as row 1.

Row 10: as row 2.

Row 11: as row 1.

Row 12: as row 1.

Row 13: as row 1.

Row 14: p1 (k8, p2, c8b, p2) rep. around ending with p1.

Row 15: as row 1.

Row 16: as row 1.

Row 17: as row 1.

Row 18: as row 14.

Row 19: as row 1.

Row 20: as row 1.

Row 21: as row 1.

Row 22: as row 14.

Row 23: as row 1.

Row 24: as row 1.

The collar of the shell is a simple garter stitch in the round.

Repeat these 24 rows until sweater measures 15" long. Break for armholes. Work in pattern on 120 (140) sts only leaving remaining sts on a spare needle or holder to be worked later.

Keeping pattern correct and working back and forth, decrease 1 st on each side on every other row after the first and before the last cable as follows:

P1, k8, p1, slip, slip and knit these 2 sts together. Work to the last 12 sts and knit 2 together then p1, k8, p1.

Continue to decrease in this manner until there are 100 (120) sts remaining. When armhole measures 8", put the center 30 sts on a holder. At the neck edge only, dec 1 st every row 4 times. Bind off remaining 20 (30) sts. Repeat for the other shoulder.

Rejoin yarn to the 120 (140) sts and work the front as for back until armholes measure 6". Place center 18 sts on a holder. At neck edge only, bind off 2 sts 2 times, then 1 st every other row 6 times. When front shoulder measures the same as the back, bind off. Repeat for the other shoulder. Sew shoulder seams together.

ARM BANDS

With 16" size 4 needles, pick up 80 sts around armholes (p 1 round, k 1 round). Repeat 2 times more. Bind off loosely.

COLLAR

With 16" size 7 needles, pick up 80 sts around neck. (p 1 round, k 1 round) repeat 4 more times. Increase 10 sts evenly spaced on the next round. Work another 10 rows in garter pattern. Collar should be approx. 3½" wide. BIND OFF VERY LOOSELY. For a loose collar, bind off on the collar, knit 1 st and *pull a loop through this st. Then knit next st and pass the loop over*. Repeat between * and *. This extra loop will give the needed ease for the collar to lay down.

This beautiful cable stitch boasts graceful scallops with intertwining links that make this shell a unique showpiece!

Chevron Chic

■ ■ ■

Chevrons have long offered a sporty slant on fashion,
as Coats & Clark's contemporary variegated vest attests.
Smartly accented with lots of visual interest,
the dramatic chevron is complemented
with cabling, ribbing, and rich colors.
The "V" stands for "very chic!"

■ **PROJECT**
Chevron Cabled Vest, by Coats & Clark

■ **SKILL LEVEL**
Intermediate

■ **SIZE**
Small (Medium, Large, X-Large, XX-Large)
Directions for Small with larger sizes in parentheses.
If there is only one figure, it applies to all sizes.

■ **FINISHED MEASUREMENTS**
Finished measurements: 36 (39, 42, 45, 49)"

■ **MATERIALS**
COATS & CLARK Red Heart TLC Essentials
MC—2 skeins Oasis
A—1 skein Country Blue
B—1 skein Aran
2 stitch holders

■ **NEEDLES**
Sizes 5 and 8 knitting needles
OR SIZE TO OBTAIN GAUGE

■ **GAUGE**
16 sts and 23 rows = 4"
TAKE TIME TO CHECK GAUGE.

1985 Workbasket

These front details show the striking interplay of the chevron with the vertical cabling banded neck and the rich variegated field of color below.

ABBREVIATIONS

beg = begin(ning); **bo** = bind off; **bpdc** = back post double crochet; **ch** = chain; **co** = cast on; **cont** = continue; **dc** = double crochet; **dec** = decrease; **eor** = every other row; **est** = established; **fpdc** = front post double crochet; **hdc** = half double crochet; **k** = knit; **lp** = loop; **psso** = pass sl st over k st; **p** = purl; **Pat** = pattern; **rem** = remaining; **rep** = repeat; **RS** = right side; **sc** = single crochet; **sk** = skip; **sl** = slip; **sst(s)** = stitch(es); **St st** = Stockinette stitch; **WS** = wrong side; ***** = repeat whatever follows the * as indicated; **[ ]** = work directions given in brackets the number of times specified.

DIRECTIONS

STITCHES / MOTIFS

BEADED RIBBING:

Row 1: (RS) [p1, k1, p1, k1, p1] across.

Row 2: (WS) [k1, p3, k1] across.

CHEVRON PATTERN:

Row 1: (RS) K across.

Row 2: (WS) [P1, k1] to last st, p 1 st.

BODY PATTERN:

Row 1: (RS) K.

Row 2 and All WS Rows: Purl across.

Row 3: (RS) [K1, p1] across.

Row 4: (WS) Rep Row 2.

NOTE

Patterns are worked with separate balls. Be certain to wrap new color around previous color to prevent holes.

BACK

With smaller needles and MC, co 71, (77, 83, 89, 95) sts.

Row 1: P1, work Row 1 of Beaded Ribbing across, p1.

Row 2: K1, work Row 2 of Beaded Ribbing across, k1.

Repeat Rows 1 and 2 for 2¾", ending with a WS Row, increasing 2 sts evenly spaced on last row—73 (79, 85, 91, 97) sts. Work in Body Pattern until piece measures 10½ (10½, 11, 11, 11½)", begin Underarm: bo 3 (3, 3, 4, 4) sts at beg of next 2 rows, then dec 1 st each side every other row 3 (3, 4, 4, 5) times— 61 (67, 71, 75, 79) sts. Work even.

When piece measures 13 (13, 13¼, 13¾, 13¾)", ending with WS row, fasten off MC, attach A. Work in Chevron Pattern for 9 rows, ending with RS row. Fasten off A, attach B; P across 23, (26, 28, 30, 32) sts, rep [between [ ] = s of WS row of Beaded Ribbing] 3 times; P across rem sts. Keeping center 15 sts in Beaded Ribbing, work even in St st until armhole measures 8¼ (8¼, 8½, 8¾, 9)". Bo 8 sts at beg of next 2 rows; bo 12 sts at beg of next 2 rows. Next Row: bo 3, (6, 8, 10, 12) sts; work in Beaded Ribbing across 15 sts; place on holder, bo rem sts.

Back of shell showing cabling and color band, which runs straight across the back.

FRONT:

With smaller needles and MC, co 71 (77, 83, 89, 95) sts. Repeat as for back until piece measures 9", ending with a WS row.

Begin Chevron: Work in est pattern across 29 (32, 35, 38, 41) sts, attach A, work Row 1 of Chevron Pattern; with another ball of MC, work across rem sts.

Next Row: With MC, P across 28 (31, 34, 37, 40) sts. With A, work Row 2 of Chevron Pattern across 17 sts. With MC, p across rem sts. Continue inc 1 st in A, (dec 1 st in MC) ea side of Chevron ea row until there are 9 rows completed, ending with RS row.

Next Row: (RS) With MC, work in est pattern to Chevron, work in A across 9 sts. Attach B, Soft White, k1, place marker, rep [between [ ]=s of WS Row of Beaded Ribbing] 3 times. Place marker, k1; with another ball of A, work in Chevron pattern across 9 sts. With MC, work in pattern across rem sts. Following chart, work until all sts are in B, keeping center 15 sts in Beaded Ribbing pattern.

At the same time, when piece measures 10½ (10½, 11, 11, 11½)", begin underarm: bo 3, (3, 3, 4, 4) sts at beg of next 2 rows, then dec 1 st ea side every other row 3 (3, 4, 4, 5) times—61 (67, 71, 75, 79) sts. Work even as established.

When armhole measures 6½ (6½, 6½, 7, 7)", ending with RS row, begin neck shaping: P across 23 (26, 28, 30, 32) sts. Work Row 2 of Beaded Ribbing across center 15 sts, then place on holder; p across

rem sts.

Next Row: K across to 3 sts before neck; k2 tog; k 2 (neck dec made). Continue dec at neck edge eor; at the same time, when armhole measures same as back to shoulder at armhole edge, bo 8 sts 1 time; 12 sts 1 time, then any rem sts.

Leaving center sts on holder, attach yarn to right neck; k2; [sl1, k1, psso], k to end. Work as for Left neck, reversing all shaping.

FINISHING

Neck: Sew right shoulder seam. With smaller needles and B, pick up 11, (11, 11, 14, 14) sts along left neck edge, work in RS pattern across 15 sts from front neck holder, 12 (12, 12, 15, 15) sts along right neck edge, 10 (10, 10, 12, 12) sts across bo sts of back to holder, work in RS pattern across 15 sts from back neck holder; pick up 9 (9, 9, 11, 11) across rem bo sts—72 (72, 72, 82, 82) sts.

Next Row: (WS) P3, then Row 2 of Beaded Ribbing around, ending K2. Work in Beaded Ribbing for 2¼", ending with RS row. Fasten off B. With A, working Row 2 of Beaded Ribbing, bo loosely with A in pattern.

Sew neck ribbing seam and left shoulder. With smaller needles and B, pick up 72 (72, 72, 77, 77) sts around armhole. Work [(WS) k1, Row 2 across, k1.

Next Row: (RS) p1, Row 1 across, p1] twice of Beaded Ribbing; fasten off B. With A, work k1, Row 2 across, k1; bo loosely in pattern.

Sew underarm seams. Weave in all loose ends; block lightly.

Pocket Panache

Lion Brand's chill-chasers in downy-soft Homespun yarn aren't just any run-of-the-mill winter wraps. The scarf has built-in hand-warmers that are both fashionable and practical. Quick, easy, and stylish!

■ **PROJECT**
Tam & Scarf with Pockets, by Lion Brand

■ **SKILL LEVEL**
Beginner

■ **SIZE**
Tam—One size fits most (10" diameter / 32" circumference)
Scarf—Measures 8" x 76", unfinished

■ **MATERIALS**
LION BRAND Homespun (each skein 6 oz)
Barrington or color of your choice
1 skein for the tam
2 skeins for the scarf

■ **NEEDLES**
16" size 8 circular needle
16" size 10 circular needle
Size 10 double-pointed needle
OR SIZE TO OBTAIN GAUGE

■ **GAUGE**
14 St sts = 4" on size 10 needle
TAKE TIME TO CHECK GAUGE.

1970 Workbasket

ABBREVIATIONS

beg = begin(ning); **dec** = decreas(e)(s)(ing); **DPNs** = double-pointed needles; **k** = knit; **p** = purl; **psso**= pass sl st over k st; **rem** = remain(s)(ing); **rep** = repeat; **rnd(s)** = round(s); **st(s)** = stitch(es); **St st** = Stockinette stitch; **tog** = together.

DIRECTIONS

STITCH EXPLANATIONS

M1 = make 1. An increase worked by lifting the horizontal thread lying between the needles and placing it onto the left needle. Work this new stitch through the back loop.

Sl 2 kwise-k1-p2sso = slip 2 stitches together knit-wise (as though to knit), knit 1, pass 2 slipped stitches over the knit stitch = centered double decrease.

TAM

Using smaller needles, loosely cast on 70 sts. Place marker to indicate beg of rnd.

Rnds 1-7: K1, p1 rib.

Rnd 8: * K2, M1, rep from * across the rnd (105 sts).

Homespun Yarn Samples

Rich in texture and blended hues, LION BRAND's Homespun yarn comes in a glorious range of colors.

Rnd 9: Change to larger needles and work in St st for 3½".

Crown: Decrease as follows (change to DPNs when necessary):

Dec Rnd 1: K 6, * sl 2 kwise-k1-p2sso, k 12, rep from * 6 more times; k6. K 1 rnd.

Dec Rnd 2: K 5, * sl 2 kwise-k1-p2sso, k 10, rep from * 6 more times; k5. K 1 rnd.

Continue decreasing in this manner every other round until 7 sts rem.

Next Rnd: K2tog around until 2 rem. Work 2 rnds on 2 sts. Break yarn and pull through remaining sts. Hide ends. Wet block tam on large dinner plate.

SCARF

With larger needles, cast on 29 sts.

Row 1: Working back and forth, k1, *p1, k1; rep from *.

Repeat Row 1 for 76". Bind off.

Finishing: Laying scarf flat, fold up 8" on each side to form pockets. Sew sides in place invisibly.

Vintage design.

Homespun Yarn Samples

Striped Sensation

■ ■ ■

Turtlenecks are toasty, but Tahki Stacy Charles'
sensational striped turtle in their Fargo yarn
veritably sizzles in red-hot reds and fiery
speckles of orange and cobalt!

■ **PROJECT**
Striped Turtleneck Sweater, by Tahki Stacy Charles

■ **SKILL LEVEL**
Advanced

■ **SIZE**
Small (Medium, Large)
Directions for Small with larger sizes in parentheses.
If there is only one figure, it applies to all sizes.

■ **MATERIALS**
TAHKI STACY CHARLES Fargo (each ball 1¾ oz. 60 yds.)
A—2 balls Multi Pink
B—1 ball Blue
C—2 balls Multi Blue
D—1 ball Orange
E—2 balls Multi Orange
F—3 (3, 4) balls Raspberry
Stitch holders

■ **NEEDLES**
Size 10½ knittng needles
Size 10 circular needle 16"
OR SIZE TO OBTAIN GAUGE

■ **GAUGE**
10 sts and 16 rows = 4" in St st with larger
needles
TAKE TIME TO CHECK GAUGE.

1975 Workbasket

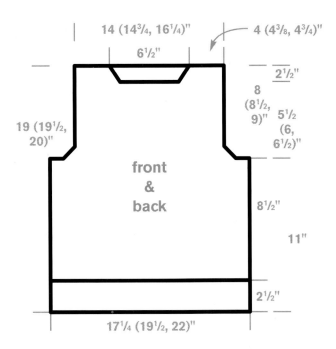

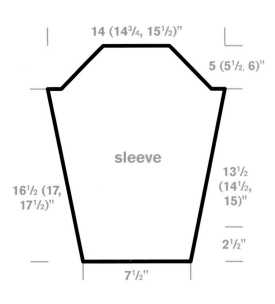

ABBREVIATIONS

beg = begin(ning); **dec** = decreas(e)(s)(ing); **DPNs** = Double-pointed needles; **k** = knit; **p** = purl; **psso**= pass sl st over k st; **rem** = remain(s)(ing); **rep** = repeat; **rnd(s)** = round(s); **RS** = right side; **st(s)** = stitch(es); **St st** = stockinette stitch; **tog** = together; **WSRC** = wrong side row completed; * = repeat whatever follows the * as indicated.

DIRECTIONS

PATTERN STITCH

Borders: Rib:

Row 1: (RS) K2, *P3, K3 *, end P3, K2.

Row 2: (WS) P2, *K3, P3 *, end K3, P2.

Body Stripes: (St st) 4 rows A, 2 rows B, 4 rows C, 2 rows D, 4 rows E, 2 rows F.

BACK

With size 10½ needle and F, cast on 43 (49, 55) sts and work even in k3, p3 rib pattern for 2½". End with wrong side row completed (End WSRC). Change to St st and work stripe sequence until piece measures 11". (End WSRC).

Shape Armhole: Maintain color sequence; bind off 2 (3, 4) sts at the beginning of the next 2 rows (always decrease as follows: at the beginning of the row, k2 tog; work to the last 4 sts, slip one as if to knit, knit 1, psso, k2.) Decrease 1 st each end every other row 2 (3, 3) times: 35 (37, 41) sts. Work even until armhole measures 8 (8½, 9)". Bind off 9 (10, 12) sts at the beginning of the next 2 rows. Place center 17 sts on holder.

FRONT

Work exactly as back until armhole measures 6 (6½, 7)". (End WSRC).

Shape Front Neck: Work 12 (13, 15) sts. Place center 11 sts on holder. Join a second ball of yarn and work remaining 12 (13, 15) sts. Decrease 1 st each neck edge every other row 3 times. Work even on each side until armhole measures 8 (8½, 9)". Bind off remaining sts.

Vintage to Vogue: Toasty turtlenecks shown, then and now—*Workbasket's* 1975 version and today's turtle in Tahki Stacy Charles' bold stripes, bold colors, and bold texture.

SLEEVES

With size 10½ needle and F, cast on 19 sts and work even in k3, p3 rib pattern for 2½".

Maintain color sequence as for back and increase 1 st each end on the 7th row and every 6th row 7 (8, 5) times, every 4th row 0 (0, 5) times; 35 (37, 39) sts. Shape cap when piece measures approximately 16 (17, 17½)", ending with same stripe as on back to armhole (end WSRC).

Shape Cap: Bind off 3 sts at the beginning of the next 2 rows. Decrease 1 st each end every other row 8 (9, 10) times, every row 2 times. Bind off all sts.

FINISHING

Block pieces to measurements. Sew shoulder seams. Sew side and sleeve seams; set in sleeves.

Neckband: With size 10 circular needle and F and with right side facing, pick up 42 (42, 48) sts evenly around neck and work in k3, p3 rib pattern for 6"; bind off loosely in pattern.

Learn How— It's Easy!

See why so many are rediscovering the ancient crafts of knitting, crocheting, and tatting. They're easy to learn and provide endless hours of quiet enjoyment and creativity!

Knitting, crochet, and tatting, like their other needlecraft cousins, are ancient crafts, and you're about to learn the basic stitches like so many women and men, girls and boys for thousands of years have done.

This section was designed for beginners and contains step-by-step diagrams with easy-to-understand instructions. Review this section for the meaning of specific terms and diagrams on specific stitches you may find in projects included in this book.

Like most crafts and hobbies, there is a simple language of terms unique to needlework. So let's start there. Following are some simple universal abbreviations used in knitting, crochet, and tatting notation. **Don't be intimidated by the list! You'll only need to learn several abbreviations to do most of the projects in this book.** But some projects will include special stitches, so those notations are also included here.

Special thanks to Coats & Clark for providing these How-To Basics.

ABBREVIATIONS

approx = approximately
beg = begin(ning)
bl = block
CC = contrasting color
ch = chain
cl r = close ring
cn = cable needle
cont = continu(e)(ing)
dc = double crochet
dec = decrease(ing)
ds = double stitch
Dtr = double treble
foll = follow(s)(ing)
incr = increase(ing)
k = knit
LH = left hand
lp = loop

MC = main color
M1 = make 1 (incr 1)
meas = measures
p = purl
P = picot
Pc st = popcorn stitch
pat(s) = pattern(s)
pm = place marker
psso = passs slip st over
rem = remain(ing)
rep = repeat
R = ring
RH = right hand
RS = right side
rw = row
sc = single crochet
sk = skip

sl = slip
sp = space
ssk = slip, slip, knit
st(s) = stitch(es)
St st = Stockinette stitch
tog = together
t-ch = turning chain
tr = treble
Tr tr = triple trebler
WS = wrong side
wyib = with yarn in back
wyif = with yarn in front
yd(s) = yard(s)
yo = yarn over
* = repeat as indicated
[ ] = repeat as indicated

How-To-Knit Basics

Knitting is enjoying an incredible resurgence today and many are discovering the enjoyment creativity and the calming effect of this needlecraft. One of the beauties of knitting is that you need only minimal equipment and you can knit almost anywhere.

EQUIPMENT

Knitting needles are used in pairs to produce a flat knitted fabric. The needles may be made of plastic, wood, steel, or alloy and range in size from 0 (2mm) to 15 (10mm) in diameter. Needles are also made in different lengths. Each project in this book will recommend the types of needles you will need.

Circular and double-pointed needles are used to produce a tubular fabric or flat rounds (such as circular shawls). Circular needles consist of two needles joined by a flexible length of plastic. Double-pointed needles are sold in sets of four or five.

Cable needles are short and double pointed, and they are used to hold the stitches temporarily when knitting cables.

Stitch holders resemble large safety pins and are used to hold stitches while they are not being worked. For example, they are often used to hold a neckline so it doesn't unravel while the front and back pieces are being joined.

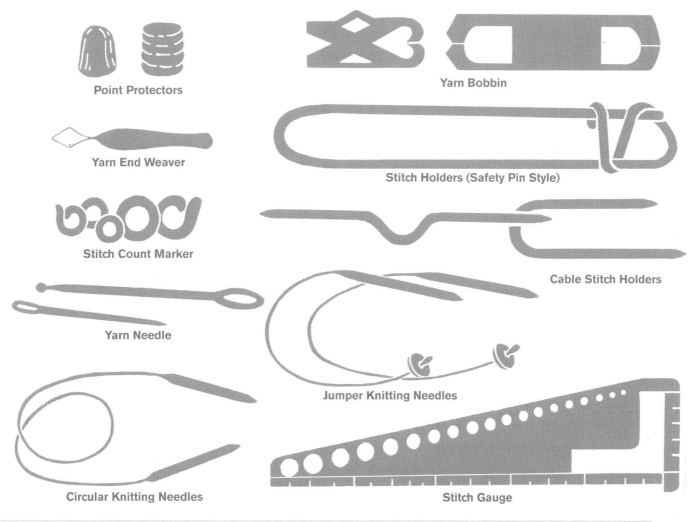

Point Protectors

Yarn End Weaver

Stitch Count Marker

Yarn Needle

Circular Knitting Needles

Yarn Bobbin

Stitch Holders (Safety Pin Style)

Cable Stitch Holders

Jumper Knitting Needles

Stitch Gauge

KNITTING YARNS

The wide array of yarns available today is nothing less than spectacular! The selection in colors, textures, twists, weights, composition, and embellishments is endless. *Vintage to Vogue's* then-and-now fashion examples underscore how exciting contemporary yarns can dramatically alter the way a basic design looks.

We recommend that you use the yarn stated in each project. It is important that you buy all the yarn needed for a project at the same time, as different dye lots can vary subtly in shading, which may show on the finished piece. Most of these yarns should be available at your local yarn shop. However, you can also order yarns featured in these projects through the manufacturer by phone or the Internet. Refer to the "Resources" section beginning on page 123 for details.

Always keep the ball band as a reference. The best way is to pin it to the gauge swatch and keep them together with any left over yarn. That way you can always check the washing instructions and have materials for repairs.

First Steps

MAKING A SLIP KNOT

A slip knot is the starting point for almost everything you do in knitting and is the basis for all casting on techniques. "Casting on" is the simple process of starting a stitch with your needles and yarn.

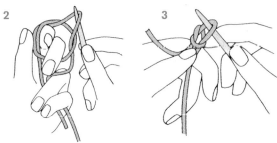

1. Wind the yarn around two fingers and over the two fingers again to the back of the first thread.

2. Using a knitting needle, pull the back thread through the front one to form a loop.

3. Pull end to tighten the loop.

HOLDING THE NEEDLES

The right needle is held as if holding a pencil. For casting on and working the first few rows, the knitted piece passes over the hand, between the thumb and the index finger.

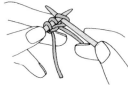

As work progresses, let the thumb slide under the knitted piece, grasping the needle from below.

The left needle is held lightly, using the thumb and index finger to control the tip of the needle.

HOLDING THE YARN

There are various methods of winding the yarn around the fingers to control the tension on the yarn and produce even stitches. In time, you may find your own favorite way, but first try the method shown here.

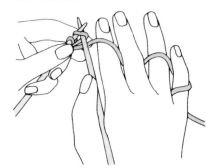

Holding the yarn in your right hand, pass under the little finger, then around the same finger, over the next finger, under the center finger, and over the index finger.

Now use the index finger to pass the yarn around the needle tip.

The yarn circled around the little finger creates the necessary tension for knitting evenly.

CASTING ON

There are two common methods of casting on: (1) Cable or *between* stitches method gives a firm neat finish and is best used before ribbing. (2) The thumb method is best for an elastic edge or when followed by rows in Garter stitch or Stockinettte stitch.

Cable Method

1. Make a slip knot about four inches from the end of the yarn.

2. Insert the right-hand needle through the slip knot and pass the yarn over the right needle.

3. Pull a loop through.

4. Place this loop on the left-hand needle.

5. Insert the right-hand needle between the two stitches on the left-hand needle. Wind yarn around the point of the right-hand needle.

6. Draw a loop through, place this loop on the left-hand needle.

Repeat steps 5 and 6 until the required number of stitches has been cast on.

Thumb Method

1. Make a slip knot about 1 yard (depending on the number of stitches required) from the end of the yarn. Hold the needle in the right hand with the ball end of the yarn over your first finger. *Wind the loose end of the yarn around the left thumb from front to back.

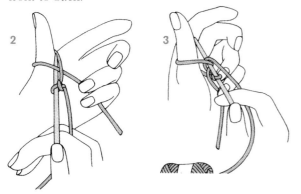

2. Insert the needle through the yarn on the thumb.

3. Take the ball end of yarn with your right forefinger over the point of the needle.

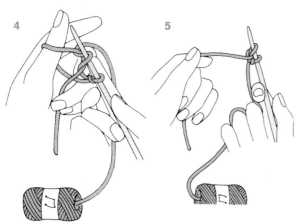

4. Pull a loop through to form the first stitch.

5. Remove your left thumb from the yarn and pull the loose end to secure the stitch.

Repeat from * until the required number of stitches has been cast on.

The Basic Stitches

KNIT STITCHES

1. Hold the needle with the cast on stitches in the left hand. With the yarn at the back of the work, insert the right-hand needle from left to right through the front of the first stitch on the left-hand needle.

2. Wind the yarn from left to right over the point of the right-hand needle.

3. Draw the yarn back through the stitch, thus forming a loop on the right-hand needle.

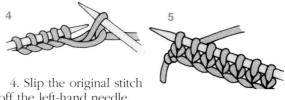

4. Slip the original stitch off the left-hand needle.

To knit a row, repeat steps 1 to 4 until all the stitches have been transferred onto the right needle.

5. Turn the work and transfer the needle with the stitches onto the left hand to work the next row.

When every row is knitted (known as Garter stitch or plain knitting), both sides of the fabric have raised horizontal ridges.

PURL STITCHES

1. With the yarn at the front of the work, insert the right-hand needle from right to left through the front of the first stitch on the left-hand needle.

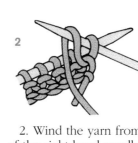 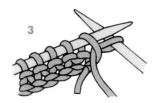

2. Wind the yarn from right to left over the point of the right-hand needle.

3. Draw a loop through onto the right-hand needle.

4. Slip the stitch off the left-hand needle.

To purl a row, repeat steps 1 to 4 until all the stitches are transferred to the right-hand needle,

then turn the work and transfer the needles to work the next row.

Purling every row creates a Garter stitch but can be slower to work than knitting every row.

STOCKINETTE STITCH

The Stockinette stitch is the most widely knitted fabric, comprised of alternate knit and purl horizontal rows. Follow the preceding instructions for Knit Stitches and Purl Stitches with each alternating row.

SINGLE RIB (k1, p1)

This technique is formed by alternately knitting a stitch then purling a stitch to create unbroken vertical lines on each side of the work. It makes a very elastic fabric that is mainly used for borders such as welts, neckbands, and cuffs. When used as an edging, rib is generally worked on a smaller size needle than the main body of the garment to keep it firm and elastic.

1. Knit the first stitch.

2. Bring the yarn forward to the front of the work between the needles and purl the next stitch.

3. Take the yarn to the back of the work between the needles and knit the next stitch.

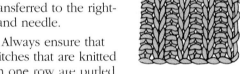

Repeat steps 2 and 3 until all stitches are transferred to the right-hand needle.

Always ensure that stitches that are knitted on one row are purled on the following row and vice versa.

How-To-Crochet Basics

Crocheting is one of the oldest needlework arts. Its name is derived from the French word "croche," meaning a hook. Even a beginner can master intricate laces and designs. Only two items are required for crocheting—a hook and thread or yarn. All crochet designs are only variations of a few basic crochet stitches.

EQUIPMENT

Crochet hooks are usually made from steel, aluminum, or plastic in a range of sizes according to their diameter. As each crochet stitch is worked separately until only one loop remains on the hook, space is not needed to hold stitches, and the hooks are made to a standard convenient length.

Crochet Hook

CROCHET YARNS & THREADS

As with knitting yarns, today's crochet threads and yarns are available in a vast array of thicknesses, twists, and finishes. It's recommended that you use the yarn stated in each project, and it's important that you buy all the yarn needed for a project at the same time, as different dye lots can vary subtly in shading, which may show on the finished piece. Most of these yarns should be available at your local yarn shop. However, you can also order yarns featured in these projects through the manufacturer, by phone or the Internet. Refer to the "Resources" section beginning on page 123 near the back of this book for details.

Always keep the ball band as a reference. Pin it to the gauge swatch and keep them together with any leftover yarn. That way you can always check the washing instructions and have materials for repairs.

HOLDING THE HOOK AND YARN

There are no hard and fast rules as to the best way to hold the hook and yarn. The diagrams below show just one method, but choose whatever way you find most comfortable. The following directions are for right-handers. Left-handers should simply reverse the process, reading left for right and right for left where applicable.

1. The hook is held in the right hand as if holding a pencil.

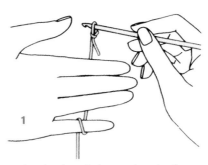

2. To maintain the slight tension in the yarn necessary for easy even working, it's helpful to arrange the yarn around the fingers of the left hand in the way shown below.

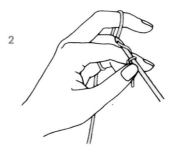

3. The left hand holds the work and at the same time controls the yarn supply. The left-hand middle finger is used to manipulate the yarn, while the index finger and thumb hold onto the work.

First Steps

Almost all crochet begins with a base of starting chain, which is a series of chain stitches, beginning with a slip knot.

MAKING A SLIP KNOT

1. Make a loop then hook another loop through it.

2. Tighten gently and slide the knot up to the hook

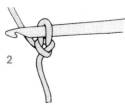

YARN OVER (yo)

Wrap the yarn from back to front over the hook to hold the yarn still and maneuver the hook. This movement of the yarn over the hook is used over and over again in crochet and is usually called "yarn over," abbreviated as "yo."

CHAIN STITCH (ch)

1. Yarn over and draw the yarn through to form a new loop without tightening up the previous one.

2. Repeat to form as many chains as required. Do not count the slip knot as a stitch.

Unless otherwise stated, when working into the starting chain always work under two strands of chain loops as shown in the diagrams.

The Basic Stitches

The following basic stitches are shown worked into a starting chain but the method is the same whatever part of the work the stitch is worked into.

SLIP STITCHES (sl st)

This is the shortest of crochet stitches and, unlike other stitches, it is not used on its own to produce a fabric. It is used for joining, shaping, and, where necessary, carrying the yarn to another part of the fabric for the next stage.

1. Insert the hook into the work (second chain from hook in diagram), yarn over and draw the yarn through both the work and loop on the hook in one movement.

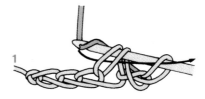

2. To join a chain ring with a slip stitch, insert the hook into the first chain, yarn over, and draw through the work and the loop on the hook.

SINGLE CROCHET (sc)

1. Insert the hook into the work (second chain from hook on starting chain), * yarn over, and draw the yarn through the work only.

2. Yarn over again and draw the yarn through both loops on the hook.

3. 1 sc made. Insert hook into next stitch; repeat from * in step 1.

HALF DOUBLE CROCHET (hdc)

1. Yarn over and insert the hook into the front of the work (third chain from hook on starting chain).

2. * Yarn over again and draw through the work only.

3. Yarn over again and draw through all three loops on the hook.

4. 1 hdc made. Yarn over, insert hook into next stitch; repeat from * in step 2.

DOUBLE CROCHET (dc)

1. Yarn over and insert the hook into the work (fourth chain from hook on starting chain).

2. * Yarn over again and draw through the work only.

3. Yarn over and draw through all two loops only.

4. Yarn over and draw through the last two loops in the hook.

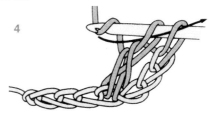

5. 1 dc made. Yarn over, insert hook into next stitch; repeat from * in step 2.

How-To-Tat Basics

Tatting is an ancient needlecraft that was practiced in Europe and the Far East for thousands of years. In the 1700s, European nobility took up tatting as a genteel artform. Decorative tatted laces and edgings were thus customarily used to decorate gowns as a fashion statement. The Pilgrims brought the needlecraft to the Colonies, and it remained popular in the United States until World War I. Today, tatting is being rediscovered, especially for teen chokers, anklets, and belts.

EQUIPMENT

A simple tool called a shuttle is used in tatting. Shuttles can be made of various materials such plastic or steel, with or without a hook at the end. The hook is especially helpful when joining rings or picots of thread, which are the basis of tatting. Tatting can also be done with a needle, but a shuttle makes it much easier.

Very simply, tatting is done by winding loops or knots of thread around a length of thread with the shuttle. Do not wind the thread beyond the edge of the shuttle. When making different motifs or patterns, count the number of turns of thread around the shuttle so you can assess the amount of thread you need for each motif. This way you won't have to do unnecessary joining of thread ends in the middle of a motif.

THREADS

Fine threads are usually used for tatting. Clark's Big Ball sizes 20, 30, and 40 are ideally suited for this work. South Maid and J. & P. Coats 'Knit-Cro-Sheen' size 10 are available in a range of lovely colors and are suitable for heavier work.

BEFORE YOU BEGIN

Tatting is composed of just a few basic techniques, such as the double stitch, rings, picots, and chains. Practice these simple techniques first to become proficient, and your work will go much faster when you begin an actual project.

ABBREVIATIONS

Tatting uses tatting and also crochet terminology. Following is a brief list of abbreviations used specifically in tatting directions.

ch = chain	**cl** = close
dc = double crochet	**ds** = double stitch
dtr = double treble	**j** = join
lp = long picot	**lr** = long ring
p(s) = picot(s)	**R** = ring
rw = reverse work	**sc** = separated
sep = separated	**smp** = small picot
sp = space	**sr** = small ring
ss = slip stitch	**tog** = together
tr = treble	* = repeat as indicated
( ) = repeat as indicated	

The Basic Stitches

THE DOUBLE STITCH (ds)

1. Let approximately 15 inches of the shuttle thread hang loose from the back of the shuttle. Hold the shuttle in the right hand and the free end of the shuttle thread between the thumb and forefinger of the left hand.

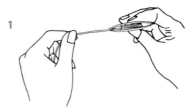

2. Bring the thread around the fingers of the left hand to form a circle. Bend the ring and little finger of the left hand to catch the thread against the palm.

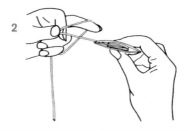

3. Pass the shuttle thread around the back of the little finger of the right hand.

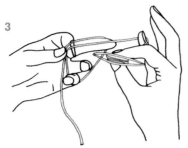

4. Move the shuttle forward, passing it under the shuttle thread and through the circle of thread.

5. Bring the shuttle back over the circle of thread and under the shuttle thread.

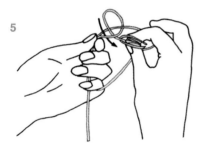

6. Drop the thread from the little finger of the right hand and draw the shuttle thread taut with a sharp jerk. As you pull with the right hand, relax the index and ring fingers of the left hand to ensure that the knot forms on the shuttle thread. Slide the loop into position between thumb and forefinger. This completes the first half of the double stitch.

7. Pass the shuttle over the circle of thread and under the shuttle thread.

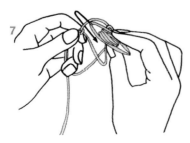

8. Draw your shuttle thread taut with a sharp jerk. As you pull with the right hand, relax the index and ring fingers of the left hand to ensure that the knot forms on the shuttle thread. Slide the loop into position next to the first half of the stitch. This completes the second half of the double stitch. Hold the double stitch between thumb and forefinger until the next stitch is made.

Note: *The shuttle thread must pull both ways through the double stitch. When the ring around the left hand becomes too small, pull through more of the shuttle thread. When the ring is completed, close it by pulling the shuttle thread tight.*

RINGS and PICOTS

1. To make a sample ring, make four double stitches. Then make the first half of a double stitch, leaving a gap of about 1/4 inch from the previous stitch. Then complete the stitch.

2. Push the whole stitch next to the previous stitch, creating an open loop that extends above the row of stitches. This open loop is called a picot.

3. Make three more double stitches (one double stitch has already been completed at the base of the picot, making four double stitches between each picot). Continue this process, making four double stitches between each picot, until you have created three picots.

4. To create a ring, connect the two shuttled ends by holding the work firmly in the left hand and drawing the shuttle thread until the first and last stitches meet, forming a ring.

Note: *The abbreviated instructions for this basic ring with three picots are: R of 4 ds, 3 ps sep by 4ds, 4ds cl. The translation: Ring of 4 double stitches, 3 picots separated by 4 double stitches, 4 double stitches closed.*

TATTING A CONNECTING CHAIN

1. A chain connects two rings and is made the same way as a ring with three picots, but the two ends are not connected to form a ring. Instead, the loose end of the chain is connected to another ring, as shown below.

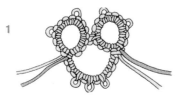

2. Working with two threads allows a wider range of patterns. You can join a second thread by using a knot to fasten in a new thread at the base of a ring. Then work the double stitches and picots over the shuttle thread in the same way your first ring was created.

TATTING A SECOND RING

1. Tat four double stitches next to the finished chain. Now instead of making a picot, join the thread to the last picot in the previous ring to connect the first and second ring. To join the picot, hold the first ring in the left hand. With the right hand, insert the shuttle end into the last picot of the first ring and pull the circle of thread through. Pull the loop large enough to insert the shuttle. Draw the shuttle through the loop and pull the shuttle thread tight. This joins the rings and takes the place of the first picot on the second ring.

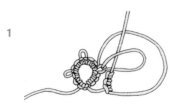

2. Continue completing the second ring and join the end at the base to close the second ring.

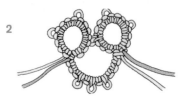

3. Continue the above process, tatting connecting chains between rings connected by shared picots.

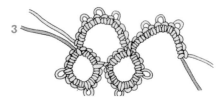

REVERSING WORK

Turn work so that the base of the ring or chain just completed faces downwards. The next ring or chain is then worked in the usual way, with the rounded edge facing upwards.

FINISHING ENDS

Make a knot to close the base of the last ring or chain. Do not cut off ends. With a single strand of thread, over sew the ends on the wrong side of the work.

Resources

The contemporary fashions in this book were designed by some of the world's top designers and yarn manufacturers, featuring some of their premiere yarns. Refer to this section for information about the companies, products, and other patterns you can purchase from these fine manufacturers, as well as other helpful information sources.

 Coats & Clark

Coats & Clark

8 Shelter Drive
Greer, SC 29650
Phone: 864.848.5610
Fax: 864.848.5609
Web site: www.coatsandclark.com

COATS & CLARK PROJECTS FEATURED IN THIS BOOK:

- Divine Duster, page 14
- Button-Front Tweed Cardigan, page 48
- Powder Puff Sweater, page 52
- Checkerboard Sweater, page 80
- Chevron Cabled Vest, page 100

Special thanks to Coats & Clark for the use of their directions and illustrations on how to knit, crochet, and tat, on pages 112 to 123. These instructions and many additional stitches may be found in Coats and Clark's *Learn How Book*, published by Lyric Books Limited, 1993.

ABOUT THE COMPANY:

Coats & Clark has long been a household name among needlecrafters. Today Coats & Clark is the largest textile/thread manufacturing company in the world, with products sold in over 150 countries.

The company was established more than 180 years ago in Paisley, Scotland, where its weavers first reproduced the rare Kashmir shawls of India. The Clark family built a thriving loom equipment business and began selling silk threads, as well.

The "Clark" part of the partnership had its start in 1806, when Napoleon blockaded Great Britain and silk was no longer available. Patrick Clark created a method of twisting cotton yarns together to produce a thread that was so strong and smooth it could be substituted for the silk. The Clarks opened the first factory for making cotton sewing thread in 1812.

In 1896, the Coats' and the Clarks' interests were consolidated, however they retained separate identities. In 1952 J. & P. Coats and the Clark Thread Co. merged to become Coats & Clark Inc.

Today the company sells a wide line of products from Red Heart® and other yarns, to crochet threads, embroidery floss, threads, zippers, trims, and other products.

PRODUCT INFORMATION:

Over the years, the product range has expanded to additionally include specialty Threads, Zippers, Tapes and Trims, Needlework Accessories, specialty Hand Knitting and Craft Yarns, Crochet Threads, and Embroidery Floss. Today major brands include Dual Duty Plus®, Red Heart®, Anchor®, J. & P. Coats, South Maid®, Susan Bates®, and Aunt Lydia®.

WEB SITE:

Coats & Clark's Web site at www.coatsandclark.com is an extensive site full of consumer and product information, in addition to an extensive offering of patterns and books, many of which are free!

MORE PATTERNS & PATTERN BOOKS:

Coats & Clark offers a wide range of CD-ROMs on Crochet, Knitting, Embroidery, and Crafts. Millions of consumers have used their "Learn How" books to teach themselves enjoyable new skills. Pattern books cover everything from afghans to apparel for the entire family, at all skill levels.

FREE STUFF!

In addition, the Coats & Clark Web site offers a long list of FREE leaflets of knitting and crochet projects, including vests, afghans, women's, men's and children's pullovers, crochet purses, home decorating, and much more!

Lion Brand Yarn Company

34 West 15th Street
New York, NY 10011
Phone: 800.258.YARN (9276)
Fax: 212.627.8154
Web site: www.LionBrandYarn.com

LION BRAND PROJECTS FEATURED IN THIS BOOK:

- Mondrian Cardigan, page 18
- Granny Squares Cardigan & Shell, page 32
- Triangle Shawl, page 56
- Heather Pullover & Tunic, page 66
- Ripple Pullover, page 76
- 60s Jiffy Crochet Vest, page 88
- Tam & Scarf with Pockets, page 104

ABOUT THE COMPANY:

At 123 years and counting, Lion Brand Yarn Company is the oldest American yarn brand. From the beginning in 1878, the Lion Brand philosophy was to provide a quality product at an affordable price. This tradition is still carried on by the fourth generation Blumenthal family members, producing yarns and patterns for today's lifestyles.

Lion Brand has long been a trendsetter in the industry. Lion Brand was the first to receive the Woolmark for hand-knitting yarns, the first to offer free patterns on the back of labels and the first to offer blended-fiber and novelty yarns at popular prices.

Each Lion Brand yarn has its own personality and is designed in a palette of colors that is appropriate to its texture and use. Lion Brand's mission is to excite and motivate needlecrafters to create handmade heirlooms that will be treasured for generations.

PRODUCT INFORMATION:

Lion Brand Yarn Company offers an expansive selection of yarns, knitting and crochet tools, patterns, books, and tools. Included is a wonderful FREE catalog that can be ordered online or over the phone.

WEB SITE:

Lion Brand's Web site www.LionBrandYarn.com offers a vast array of products, patterns, information, helpful tips, and even a gallery of customer projects. Lion Brand's site is very user-friendly and offers a long list of free downloadable patterns.

MORE PATTERNS & PATTERN BOOKS:

Lion Brand offers a wide range of books on crochet, knitting, crafts, tools, yarns, needles, and patterns.

FREE STUFF!

In addition, the Lion Brand's Web site offers numerous FREE patterns, which are downloadable.

BERROCO

Berroco, Inc.

14 Elmdale Road
P.O. Box 367
Uxbridge, MA 01569-0367
Phone: 800.343.4948
Fax: 508.278.2461
Web site: www.berroco.com

BERROCO PROJECTS FEATURED IN THIS BOOK:

- Timeless Tee, page 10
- Ribbed Pullover with Collar & Cuffs, page 22
- Button Cardigan with Fluff Collar & Cuffs, 42
- Fringed Scarf, Cap, & Mittens, page 58

ABOUT THE COMPANY:

Berroco's story begins in the year 1810 when the great-great-great-grandfather of Warren Wheelock, Berroco's president today, opened the first of the Wheelock mills in rural Massachusetts, one of the first in the fledgling United States to produce woolen cloth. He began an enterprise that would grow and change and endure through six generations. Over the years, the Stanley Woolen Company mills sold to such manufacturers as Evan Picone, Perry Ellis, Brooks Brothers, and Hager.

In 1968, the Wheelock family formed a new handknitting subsidiary called Stanley Berroco, a name forged from the names of three business associates. This new firm grew to become one of the largest importers and wholesalers of handknitting yarns, patterns, and supplies in the United States. Importing yarns from the United Kingdom, Switzerland, Germany, France, Italy, New Zealand, Japan, Brazil, and Uruguay, Berroco also produces a full range of handknitting books and patterns.

Berroco patterns and yarns have been featured in such magazines as *Woman's Day, Family Circle, Redbook, Vogue Knitting, Knitters, Knitting Digest,* and *McCall's*. In 1995, Berroco became a US distributor of top-quality Inox and Clover knitting needles rounding out their offering to the handknitter.

The year 1992 brought further change to the company. Warren Wheelock, president of Berroco since 1987, created the Handeze Glove Division, becoming the master distributor of the Handeze glove in the craft industry.

Operating on the site of one of the Wheelock family's original woolen mills, Berroco, Inc., continues the family tradition of changing with the needs of the times to provide top-quality products.

PRODUCT INFORMATION:

Berroco offers a wide range of products from their mainstay in yarns, including a lovely array of specialty and exotic yarns, books, tools, knitting needle, patterns, and the Handeze glove, manufactured by the Handeze Glove Division.

WEB SITE:

Berroco's Web site, www.berroco.com, provides a wide range of information, books, products, and patterns, including numerous FREE patterns.

MORE PATTERNS & PATTERN BOOKS:

Berroco's offers a very extensive online pattern library of both FREE and retail patterns and pattern books. Furthermore, patterns are divided by skill levels, yarn types, or fashion categories, such as women's, men's, children, home decorating, etc.

FREE STUFF!

Berroco features one of the most extensive lines of FREE patterns. In addition, it also offers a FREE online newsletter that contains product, how-to and pattern information for consumers.

Tahki Stacy Charles, Inc.

8000 Cooper Ave. Building 1
Glendale, NY 11385
Phone: 800.338.YARN (9276)
Fax: 718.326.5017
Web site: www.tahkistacycharles.com

TSC PROJECTS FEATURED IN THIS BOOK:

- Casca Sage Shag Pullover, page 6
- Scarlet Shag Shell, page 26
- Loose-knit Red Pullover, page 38
- Striped Fuzzy Sweater, page 72
- Scoopneck Sweater, page 92
- Striped Turtleneck Sweater, page 108

ABOUT THE COMPANY:

Stacy Charles Inc. and Tahki Imports LTD. merged on January 10, 2000. The new company became known as Tahki Stacy Charles, Inc. Stacy Charles, Inc. was originally launched in 1984 as a high-end luxury and novelty yarn supplier and formed a longstanding relationship with the world-renowned Filatura Di Crosa Mill. To this day, the brand names of Filatura Di Crosa and S. Charles Collezione are synonymous with superior quality and fashion.

Tahki Imports LTD. was established in 1968 and became known for its classic and quality yarns imported from Ireland, England, Greece, France, and Italy. Classic yarns like Donegal Tweed, Cotton Classic, and New Tweed continue to be mainstays for the company.

Today, TSC offers classic yarns at value prices, as well as luxurious and fashion-forward novelty yarns and fashions.

PRODUCT INFORMATION:

Tahki Stacy Charles distributes an extensive line of yarns from all over the world, including Tahki Yarns, Austermann, Filatura di Crosa, and S. Charles Collezione. TSC also offers a wonderful line of patterns and pattern books that feature international and classic European and American styles.

WEB SITE:

TSC's Web site, www.tahkistacycharles.com, provides in-depth information about their extensive product line, numerous pattern books, and a directory of shops in each state that sells TSC yarns. In addition, needlecrafters can sign up to receive a FREE pattern.

MORE PATTERNS & PATTERN BOOKS:

Tahki Stacy Charles sells numerous pattern books, featuring styles from around the work, especially Europe and the United States. Individual projects featured in each book can be viewed on the Web site.

FREE STUFF!

Visitors to TSC's Web site can sign up for a FREE pattern.

Cascade Yarns

1224 Andover Park East
Tukwila, WA 98188
Phone: 800.548.1048
Fax: 888.855.9276
Web site: www.cascadeyarns.com

CASCADE PROJECTS FEATURED IN THIS BOOK:

- Multicolor Bulky Cardigan, page 28
- Ivory Turtleneck, page 36
- Fleur-de-Lis Purse, page 62
- Sweater Coat, page 84
- Cabled Shell with Yoke, page 96

ABOUT THE COMPANY:

Cascade Yarns offers a very wide selection of yarns from all over the world, including:

- Alpaca/wool and alpaca/cotton blends from the Andes Mountains of Peru.
- Kid mohair/silk blends from the spinners of Italy.
- Fabulous baby yarns from the gifted spinners of England.
- Many brands of yarns with exotic names, such as Indulgence, Lana D'Oro, Cherub, Pastaza, Sierra, King Cole, Magnum, Confetti, Merino, and Madil.

Cascade yarns also features other needlecraft product lines, such as Jean Greenhouse's many whimsical knitting project including "Little Dumpling Dolls," clowns, toys, hedgehogs, and other animals.

PRODUCT INFORMATION:

Cascade Yarn's Web site, www.cascadeyarn.com, features numerous types of yarns from all over the world and includes close-up photographs of the colors, textures, and weights of the yarns. In addition, Cascade offers an online service in which consumers can find the nearest store that sells each brand. Cascade's site also includes an extensive offering of patterns.

MORE PATTERNS & PATTERN BOOKS:

Find a wide array of pattern offerings featuring many different types of yarns and styles from around the world.

Handy Hands, Inc.

577 N 1800
Paxton, IL 60957
Phone: 217.379.3802
Fax: 800.617.8626
Web site: www.hhtatting.com

HANDY HANDS PROJECTS FEATURED IN THIS BOOK:

- Tatted Choker & Earrings, page 46
- Tatted Bridal Garter, page 70

ABOUT THE COMPANY:

Handy Hands specializes specifically in tatting and offers a wonderful online and printed catalog, featuring all things tatting, including hundreds of books and a wide array of tools and supplies. The catalog also contains books, tools, and supplies for lace crochet, lace knitting, and bobbin lace.

The back section of the catalog has a special treat: A wide selection of shuttles, both decorative and functional, in all types of imaginative shapes, colors, and materials. Included are exotic shuttles made of everything from water buffalo horn to bone, embossed sterling silver to bronze, abalone to Mother of Pearl, and many types of colorful stones and colorfully dyed woods. You'll want to start tatting just so you can buy a beautiful shuttle!

PRODUCT INFORMATION:

Handy Hands provides nearly everything needed for tatting: shuttles, needles, tools, yarns, books, and other information, as well as tools and materials for other needlecrafts, such as bobbin lace-making and crocheting.

MORE PATTERNS:

Handy Hands online catalog features hundreds of how-to books from beginner to advanced tatting projects and patterns.

FREE STUFF!

Go to Handy Hands, Web site, www.hhtatting.com, for FREE tatting projects, wonderful how-to basics, complete with photographs, and even a question-and-answer service. You can also subscribe to an inexpensive newsletter service.

Helpful Web Sites

Visit these Web sites for more helpful information:

- Craft Yarn Council of America
  www.craftyarncouncil.com

- Crochet Guild of America
  www.crochet.com

- The Knitters Guild of America
  www.tkga.com

- The National Needlework Association
  www.tnna.org

- American Quilter's Society
  www.aqsquilt.com

- American Sewing Guild
  www.asg.org

- Hobby Industry Association
  www.i-craft.com

- Home Sewing Association
  www.sewing.org

- Sew Young/Sew Fun
  www.sewyoungsewfun.com

- The Knitting Needle
  www.knittingneedle.com

- Tatting and Design
  www.tatting.co.uk

Helpful Magazines

- *Cast On Magazine*
  www.wellroundedknitter.com

- *Knitters Magazine*
  www.knittinguniverse.com

- *Interweave Knits Magazine*
  www.interweave.com

- *Knitting Digest*
  www.knittingdigest.com

- *Knit 'N Style*
  www.knitnstyle.com

- *Vogue Knitting*
  www.vogueknitting.com

- *Family Circle Easy Knitting*
  www.fceasyknitting.com

Fashions and Accessories You Can Create Yourself

Design & Knit the Sweater of Your Dreams
by J. Marsha Michler

Now you can learn to design and knit sweaters you will want to wear again and again! J. Marsha Michler expertly guides you through three main subject areas of design and construction: creating pattern stitches and colorworking; sweater shapes and styles; and how to fit a sweater. Includes directions for designing four styles of sweaters, along with instructions for 18 different sweaters. You will also find helpful hints, diagrams, and detailed photos that will assist you in making the sweater of your dreams.
Softcover • 8⅛x10-⅞ • 144 pages

100 color photos & 75+ diagrams
Item# DKSYD • $21.95

Easy Knits
By Zoe Mellor

Presented in an easy-to-use format, *Easy Knits* stands op at any page required, allowing you to concentrate on or step at a time. You'll also find 10 exciting new projects with which to practice your skills and create useful, fun clothes, bags and gifts. Great for beginners.

Softcover w/spiral • 7½ x 7½ • 64 pages
50 color photos
Item# 32477 • $11.99

The Knitting Stitch Bible
by Maria Parry-Jones

Whether you are just learning how to knit or you have been doing it for years, you will find this book to be an invaluable resource. With detailed instructions for 250 different knitting stitches and more than 250 illustrations to guide you through each step, you will learn to create beautiful and individual hand-knitted garments.

Hardcover W/Concealed Spiral • 6⅛x8 • 256 pages
250+ color illus.
Item# KNSB • $29.95

Adventures With Polarfleece®
A Sewing Expedition
by Nancy Cornwell

Nancy Cornwell will lead you on a sewing expedition. Explore and discover endless project possibilities for the entire family. Sew a collection of 15 projects for play, work, fashion, comfort, and warmth. The heart of a falle away sewer will soon be recaptured and new sewers wi be intrigued and inspired.

Softcover • 8½ x 11 • 160 pages
200 color photos • 150 color illus.
Item# AWPF • $19.95

Knitting in the Fast Lane
More than 35 Projects for All Skill Levels
by Christina L. Holmes and Mary Colucci

You'll be inspired too when you learn how fast and easy it is to create these 35 fashionable and fun knitting projects such as afghans, ponchos, pullovers, scarves, jackets, vests, evening bags, and much more. Features a skill-level indicator for each project and tips for working with textured yarns, plus a handy reference guide to basic stitches and a list of resources for yarns and needles.

Softcover • 8¼ x 10⅞ • 128 pages
185 illus. • 50 color photos
Item# KNTFL • $21.95

Handmade Bags
How to Design, Create, and Embellish Beautiful Bags
by Terence Terry

Now you'll always have the perfect handbag to match every outfit with this great new project book! Featuring innovative ideas for creating everything from simple sequined felt bags to ornate leather designs and tote ba to a backpack and wedding bag. No matter what your skill level, you'll be able to follow these step-by-step instructions, helpful tips, shortcuts, and colorful photographs to create a handbag for every occasion.

Softcover • 8¼x8¼ • 128 pages
400+ color illus.
Item# HNDBG • $21.95

World of Knitted Toys
by Kath Delmeny

Teaches how to use knitting techniques to create delightful children's toys. Includes templates and 50+ different designs.

Softcover • 7½ x 10½ • 128 pages
48 color photos • 40 b&w illusrations
Item# 41044 • $14.99

The Cat & Dog Lovers' Idea Book
by Gail Green

Learn how to make dozens of creative projects, including toys, collars, treats, and wearables, for those special anim friends in your life. Author Gail Green will show you ho to use techniques such as rubber stamping, cross-stitch, painting, knitting, fabric applique, sewing, and decoupa to combine your love of crafting with your love of cats and dogs.

Softcover • 8¼ x 10⅞ • 112 pages
150 color photos
Item# PETLB • $17.95